ALSO BY STEPHEN MANSFIELD

Never Give In:
The Extraordinary Character of Winston Churchill

Faithful Volunteers:
The History of Religion in Tennessee

Then Darkness Fled:
The Liberating Philosophy of Booker T. Washington

More Than Dates and Dead People:
Recovering a Christian View of History

Forgotten Founding Father:
The Heroic Life of George Whitefield

THE FAITH

of

GEORGE W. BUSH

THE FAITH

of

GEORGE W. BUSH

STEPHEN MANSFIELD

Jeremy P. Tarcher / Penguin
a member of
Penguin Group (USA) Inc.

Most TARCHER/PENGUIN books are available at special quantity discounts for bulk purchase for sales promotions, premiums, fund-raising, and educational needs. Special books or book excerpts also can be created to fit specific needs. For details, write or telephone Penguin Group (USA) Inc. Special Markets, 375 Hudson Street, New York, NY 10014.

Jeremy P. Tarcher/Penguin
a member of
Penguin Group (USA) Inc.
375 Hudson Street
New York, NY 10014
www.penguin.com

This book is being published jointly by Strang Communications and Penguin Group (USA) Inc.

An application to register this book for cataloging has been submitted to the Library of Congress. International Standard Book Number: 1-58542-309-2

Printed in the United States of America
5 7 9 10 8 6

This book is printed on acid-free paper

To

LIEUTENANT COLONEL ELDON L. MANSFIELD,

U.S. ARMY (RETIRED)

CONTENTS

*Midway along the journey of our life
I woke to find myself in a dark wood,
For I had wandered off from the straight path.*

*How hard it is to tell what it was like,
This wood of wilderness, savage and stubborn
The thought of it brings back all my old fears.*

*A bitter place! Death could scarce be bitterer.
But if I would show the good that came of it
I must talk about things other than the good.*

DANTE ALIGHIERI
THE DIVINE COMEDY (I.1–6)

A higher authority: George W. Bush bows his head in prayer before speaking during a service at the Second Baptist Church in Houston, Texas, on Sunday, March 7, 1999.

INTRODUCTION

I t is too early to know how history will judge the presidency of George W. Bush. To guess at the legacy of a sitting president is a dangerous game. History is, after all, a mysterious lady who often misbehaves, who delights in going against pattern; rarely is this more evident than in American politics.

Still, the past shines enough light to allow some certainties. We can be sure, for example, that history will remember this president for the John Quincy Adams parallel. That our current president is the son of an earlier chief executive will always be discussed in light of John Adams, our second president, having been the father of our sixth. Historical memory loves simple parallels, and this one is too tempting to pass up.

There can also be no doubt that this president will be

remembered as the man in the White House on September 11, 2001. The unprecedented terrorist acts on that day and the subsequent invasions of Afghanistan and Iraq will frame a large part of Bush's legacy no matter what else he does. Had Franklin Roosevelt died just weeks after Pearl Harbor, he would still be remembered as the president on December 7, 1941, for the "Day of Infamy" speech, and for his actions immediately after the Japanese attack. So it will be with George W. Bush.

There is another likely pillar of George W. Bush's legacy that, surprisingly, it is not too early in his presidency to consider seriously. This is the matter of his religious faith and his attempts to integrate faith as a whole into American public policy. It is here that we come to one of the most unique characteristics of the Bush presidency and very possibly to one of the most defining issues of our time.

—⁓—

George W. Bush entered the presidency sounding an unapologetically religious tone. On his very first day in office, he called for a day of prayer and cut federal spending on abortion. He speaks of being called to the presidency, of a God who rules in the affairs of men, and of the United States owing her origin to Providence. Americans have had opportunity to know more about the president's conversion, prayer life, what Bible he reads, what devotional he uses, and who his spiritual influences are than they have ever known of any other president. In no previous administration has the White House hosted so many weekly Bible studies and prayer meetings, and never have religious leaders been more gratefully welcomed.

He has shared Scripture with the prime minister of England, discussed the cross with the president of Russia, knelt in prayer with the president of Macedonia, and told the leader of Turkey that the two would do well together because they both believe in "the Almighty."[1] Moreover, President Bush has attempted to use faith and faith-based institutions to solve the nation's problems in a way that is new in recent American memory and may bring, particularly if he is allowed a second term, a transformation of American social policy.

Bush's personal journey of faith is a winding road, not unusual in an age of baby-boomer spirituality. He attended Episcopal and Presbyterian churches until he married and through his wife's influence became a Methodist. The seeds of faith were planted, and he experienced what he calls "stirrings," but there was no single moment of spiritual awakening. Then came business failures, seasons of excessive drinking, and a marriage that began showing signs of strain. As midlife approached, he took the now-famous walk on a Maine beach with Billy Graham, who asked him if he was "right with God." He was not, and he knew it, but his time with Graham made him aware of his need. Bush joined a businessmen's Bible study in Midland, and before long his friends noted something different about him. Asked who his favorite philosopher was during his presidential campaign, he quickly answered with the phrase that told the story: "Christ, because He changed my heart."[2]

Yet, Bush's Christ rules the world as well as the heart. He is, as Bush attests in his autobiography, the author of a "divine plan that supersedes all human plans."[3] As the president-elect said in his inaugural address, it is God "who fills time and eternity with His purpose."[4] The individual is obligated to this purpose, as is the state. And how does government fulfill the purpose of God? The answer from Bush is unclear, but the implication—one that unsettles those who desire to preserve a broad separation of church and state—is that institutions of faith "have an honored place in our plans and in our laws."[5] If the presidency is a "bully pulpit" as Teddy Roosevelt claimed, no one in recent memory has pounded that pulpit for religion's role in government quite like the forty-third president.

Nevertheless, Bush has resisted the role of "Preacher in Chief," and his statements often seem to belie his own evangelical brand of faith. Within a week of the September 11 terrorist attacks on New York and Washington, the president spoke at an Islamic center and called Islam a religion of peace.[6] He has been hesitant to say that Jesus is the only way to God, though he once expressed this belief to a Jewish reporter and ignited a powder keg of controversy. And, much to the consternation of some conservative Christians, he is attempting to engage mosques and synagogues as well as churches in his faith-based initiatives.

The president's focus on religion has launched not only a national debate but also an entire subculture. E-mails ricochet throughout the country filled with the latest urban legends: The president visits a hospital and kneels in prayer with the stumps of a decorated soldier in his hands. The president notes a forlorn student on a college campus he is touring and stops to lead the youth to faith. Or, negatively, the president is secretly planning to destroy Jefferson's wall of separation between church and state in order to build the Televangelist Republic of His Dreams. Websites shriek in offense or approval, the campus Starbucks is filled with indignation or caffeinated joy, and radio talk shows thunder their response in the marketplace of ideas.

Without doubt, some of the hubbub about Bush's faith is rooted in an ignorance of history. As Harry Truman often said, "There is nothing new in the world except the history you don't know."[7] Not knowing our history makes Bush's faith seem out of place. Consider the president's statement about his sense of calling: "As it has been a kind of destiny that has thrown me upon this service, I'll hope that my undertaking is designed to answer some good purpose...I'll rely, therefore, confidently on Providence, which has preserved and been bountiful to me."[8] These are the kind of sentiments Bush often expresses in his speeches. But the words are not his. They were written by George Washington of his own first steps into leadership over two centuries ago.

The fact is that George W. Bush is not unique as a president because he speaks openly of religion. All American presidents have done so, and it has become part of our national lore. In the first century and a half of our history, most Americans were religious and understood their lives and their country in religious terms. By the early decades of the twentieth century, however, religion had declined as an influence in the United States, but presidents still spoke religiously of the nation as a nod to a Christian memory and as an attempt to baptize the American culture of their day.

Scholars like Robert Bellah and Sidney Mead have called this "civil religion," a kind of American Shinto, an attempt to weave American ideals into a secular religion of the state.[9] It is religious language torn from its original context and applied to the American experience. To some it is idolatrous; to others it is a necessary body of unifying sentiments. It is perhaps best exemplified by the speeches of John F. Kennedy, who quoted more Scripture in his speeches than any president up to that time but carefully applied their meaning to the Americanism of the early 1960s.

In the years since Kennedy, we have had presidents who seemed to possess profound religious convictions beyond a mere religion of the state. More than a few of these, though, have had difficulty allowing those convictions to inform their policies or, in some cases, even to inform their personal ethics. Richard Nixon was an ardent Quaker who boasted of his relationship with Billy Graham and yet gave us the ethical culture of Watergate. Jimmy Carter claimed to be born again and even taught Sunday school during his White House years, yet he seemed to erect a wall of separation between faith and practice when it came to being president. Ronald Reagan claimed a vital Christian faith and sense of mission, though he rarely went to church and his wife's dabbling in astrology made skeptics of many. And not least, Bill Clinton, despite serious wrongdoing while in office, claimed not only to be a Baptist believer but also often wept unashamedly in church and spoke repeatedly of the need for religious values in American life. Clearly, each of these men subscribed to religious values and believed that America would be a better country if her citizens did the same.

Yet, rarely did any of these men attempt to apply the power of religion to the responsibilities of the federal government. Never did they contend, for example, that poverty is related to a crisis of faith and then propose policies for the abolition of poverty that involved religious institutions as George W. Bush has done. Their style was more to speak of faith at a prayer breakfast but seek national solutions either in pragmatic experimentation or in ideologies of the Left or the Right.

What distinguishes the presidency of George W. Bush thus far is not just the openness with which he has discussed his personal conversion and spiritual life, nor simply the intensity of his public statements about faith. Rather, he is set apart both by the fact that he seems to genuinely believe privately what he says publicly about religion—when Americans are more used to religious insincerity from their leaders—and by the fact that he seeks to integrate faith with public policy at the most practical level.

This drive originates, certainly, in Bush's own spiritual transformation. But there is more here than evangelistic fervor, more than one converted man unable to rest until his fellow man experiences the same. Instead, George W. Bush was influenced after his conversion by thinkers who understood the Christian message as both personal and public, as a power for the heart as well as a plan for a nation. This may well be what most distinguishes the Bush approach to public faith among American presidents, and it may well be what will most shape his presidency for another four years, should the voters—and his God—allow.

Whatever the future, the faith of George W. Bush has been of consuming interest to Americans. Stories on the subject have appeared in magazines as diverse as *Esquire, Spin, Charisma & Christian Life, Christianity Today, Vanity Fair, Atlantic Monthly,* and *Newsweek.* Documentaries on PBS and A&E television networks have fed this fervor, as have articles in dozens of the nation's leading newspapers. This search for answers is understandable. What does the president believe, and what will it mean for the nation? Is he building a theocracy? Has his faith transformed him from a man who once could barely read a teleprompter into a man who does not need one? What does he believe about the separation of church and state? What is the connection between his faith and what some are calling his "leadership genius"? Are his policies regarding the Middle East shaped by an interpretation of the Bible that calls for unqualified support for Israel? Does he believe that history will crash to a halt in a final apocalyptic battle somewhere just north of Jerusalem?

What follows in these pages is an attempt to answer such questions by examining George W. Bush's faith both as it entered progressively into his mind and heart and as it currently shapes the affairs of his administration. There is no attempt to press a political agenda, nor is there a desire to capture Bush for one theological stream or another. Rather, there is an underlying belief that to understand the man you must first understand what is, as Paul Tillich said, of "ultimate concern" to him. This is the goal here: to know what is of ultimate concern to George W. Bush. It is a theological question and must, therefore, be answered by examining what Bush believes in order to understand who he is and how he intends to lead.

An underlying assumption of this book is that a man's religion permeates all he does whether he knows it or not. What he believes works itself out practically in his life, so there is a connection between his view of grace and his garden, between his idea of Providence and his way of parenting.

So it is with the president. The approach here assumes that there is a relationship between the president's boots and his prayer life, between his roots in West Texas and his response to the 9/11 disaster. To understand Bush's faith requires more than understanding his conversion alone, as though it hovers over the landscape of his life in a disconnected fashion. It requires knowing his style, his culture, the spiritual soil from which he grew, the manhood of the man.

Finally, there is also a vital belief represented here that there can be beauty in a religion not our own. Whether or not we agree with everything the president believes, we can still marvel at a man inspired by something beyond himself. Perhaps we must, in our age, recover the ability to be at home in the presence of conviction, even a conviction other than one we share. It is in this broad and robust spirit that we turn to consider the faith of George W. Bush.

Photo Credit: AP Photo/Harry Cabluck

His turn: The Texas governor and first lady at their second-term inauguration in Austin, Texas, January 19, 1999.

CHAPTER ONE

A Charge to Keep

It was not the Longhorns, the Aggies, or the Dallas Cowboys they were thinking about that day in Texas. Though football is nearly the state religion, Texans had something else on their minds. And they were not worrying about the price of crude. Oil seemed to be selling just fine. No, on that day in January of 1995, most Texans were thinking one thing: *Today George W. Bush will be inaugurated as governor of our state.*

He had done it. Very few thought he would. They had laughed when he announced his candidacy. Columnist Molly Ivins called him "Shrub," and even his friends chuckled when someone called him just another "rich son of a Bush." But he surprised them all, even his parents, and defeated the extremely popular incumbent, Ann Richards. He would become only the second Republican governor of Texas in the nearly 120 years since Reconstruction.

For "Dubya," the day was a blitz of events, one stacked upon the other. He was distracted as he dressed that morning; the speech Karl Rove had been writing for him played itself in a loop through his mind. There had been last-minute changes in wording, and since delivering speeches still was not his strong suit, he wanted to get it right. The speech would only last ten minutes, but it meant so much.

He was aware but not fully engaged when his father came to him and pressed a pair of cuff links into his hands. He knew what they were and probably showed some gratitude. But it may have been forced. He was still in a bit of a haze and had not really grasped the full meaning of the moment. Then, as they left the capitol to attend a prayer breakfast at a nearby church, his mother put a note in his hand. Again, there were thanks and a hug but no sense of the weightiness he would come to attach to it all later.

Then, there was the limo ride to the church and the waiting crowd. He waved as he walked toward the door, shook hands with well-wishers as he entered, and sat in silence once he found his seat. There was the usual business of such an event: the greetings, the songs, and the readings from the Bible. His mind wandered. Perhaps it all was moving too fast for him. Perhaps he wanted to remember the whole day, and it was already becoming a blur. He rehearsed the morning in his mind; perhaps that was when he recalled the note he had quickly shoved into his pocket. The preacher warmed to his text as George W. pulled the envelope from his pocket and began to read. And the tears came.

—⚬—

Another day, another year, another Texas city: It is 1943. The place is a hot, dusty air base near Corpus Christi. The Second World War is in full fury, and the United States is training recruits and shipping them abroad as fast as they can be readied. It is the ninth of June, and a graduation has just taken place at this busy airfield. Three figures are standing together in the brutal Texas sun. One is nearly six and a half feet tall and every bit of 250 pounds. There is a woman, much shorter than the other two and clearly the larger man's wife, with a noble grace already etching itself in her face. Then there is the beaming one, the tall, underweight seaman second class who has just received his navy pilot's wings. He is barely twenty years old.

The larger man, obviously the father of the new pilot, reaches into his pocket to take hold of something small, which he then presents without ceremony to his son. It is a set of gold cuff links. The son knows their meaning, for he has come to understand the ways of his father, who is not an overly expressive man. "My father is proud of me," he senses, "and these are the symbols of his joy at this wonderful and fearful moment of my life."

The boy treasures the gift and, even more, his father's pride. He thinks of it later when he is shot down over the Pacific Ocean. He remembers it when he studies at Yale, runs an oil company, wins a seat in Congress, heads the CIA, and becomes vice president and then president of the United States. And he thinks of his father and the gift the day his oldest son, George W., becomes the governor of Texas. They are his most prized possession, but it is time to pass them on.[1]

—⁂—

George W. Bush has not heard much of the sermon. Yet, the preacher must think he is doing very well. The governor-elect is in tears, after all. The sermon must be a hit.

But it is the note in his hand that has undone the newly elected governor. It is from his father, the former president.

"These cuff links are my most treasured possession," the older man has written, and he invokes that June day in 1943 when his own father first gave them. "I want you to have them now," the note says, and then the father speaks of the son "receiving his wings" on this inauguration day, of how he understands the younger man's excitement, and how he will be a fine governor. It is, in a sense, a blessing—the kind fathers have given their sons for generations.[2]

There is more in the note, however, and through the years George W. would rehearse each word again and again. But it is the last line that sticks, that he will never forget, that now moves him to weep.

Having expressed his love, his pride, and his confidence, the father writes in closing to the son: "Now, it is your turn."

Throughout the years, the Bush family has been reticent to speak of itself with words like *legacy*, *dynasty*, or, certainly, *empire*. They prefer to talk in terms of trust, destiny, and faith. But there is little question that what passed between former President George Herbert Walker Bush and his governor-son was more than jewelry and a note of encouragement. It was, as one scholar has written, "a symbolic passing of the torch."[3]

Clearly, the father was attempting to connect the son to something that had come before and that might sustain him in the days ahead. All families are defined by their stories. It is the oft-repeated tale that fashions the family culture and, if the stories are inspiring enough, fashions the family sense of purpose. The Bush heritage contains stories of the kind to fashion a sense of destiny, and if we are going to understand the faith of George W. Bush, we must first consider how his family history may have shaped his beliefs.

—⁂—

It is hard to say what part of the Bush legacy most inspired George W., but there is certainly fuel for the imagination in the tale. There were, for example, the dreamer/adventurers. Obediah Bush of Vermont is one of these, a man who left his home during the War of 1812, became a schoolmaster, then caught gold fever and left for California during the Gold Rush of 1849. Two years later, he tried to return home to reclaim his family and take them west. He died in the attempt, though, and was buried at sea, leaving his wife and seven children alone in Rochester, New York. Though his dreams were unfulfilled, he left the legacy of a visionary romantic for those who bore the family name.

There were also philosopher/poets in the Bush saga. The second of Obediah's seven children was one of these, a child named James who was born so sickly the doctor told his mother, "You better knock him in the head, for if he lives he will never amount to anything."[4] The child's mother, Harriet, was in a grand tradition of stubbornness that would survive her, and she determined to nurse the child to health. She did. Sixteen years later, the boy had not only lived but also developed into the kind of man Yale College eagerly wanted to admit.

There is a description of James Bush while he was at Yale, and had it not been written in 1907, one might suspect the author of reading the characteristics of later Bushes back into the lives of their ancestors. "His classmates speak of him," wrote William Barrett, a family friend, "as tall and slender in person, rather grave of mien, except when engaged in earnest conversation or good-humored repartee; ever kind and considerate and always a gentleman—still, very strong in his likes and dislikes. He made many friends. Anxious to make the most of his opportunities, he ranked high in his studies. Fond of athletics, he achieved considerable reputation as an oarsman, rowing stroke in his class crew. He was also quite noted as a high jumper."[5]

James was possessed of a deeply spiritual nature and determined to become a Presbyterian minister. The needs of his family prevailed, though, and to support them he decided to study law. He was admitted to the bar and opened an office in Rochester. Not too long after, James fell hard in love with a woman of renowned beauty, Sarah Freeman, and she agreed to marry him. Their happiness did not last long, however, for she died of fever a mere eighteen months after the wedding.

James was devastated, and, as often happens with the grieving, his mind turned to the spiritual. He decided to give up the practice of law and become an Episcopal priest. In time, he was ordained by the bishop of New York and took a parish in New Jersey, where he served for ten years.

Love came twice for the Rev. Bush. He met and married a woman with the same name as his mother, Harriet. She was a descendant of the Samuel Prescott who rode with Paul Revere, and the editor/poet James Russell Lowell said of her, "She possessed the finest mind and was the most brilliant young woman of my day."[6]

James' romantic soul had absorbed his father's sense of adventure, and when an opportunity came his way to serve as chaplain on a risky voyage to South America, he eagerly took it. The story is told in Rev. Bush's paper "The Trip of Monadnock," which he read before the Concord Lyceum in 1886. The episode is worth recounting here because it gave the Bush family their guiding motto.

During the voyage, a fire started near the magazine, where the explosives were kept. The captain, Mr. Franklin, leapt into the hold to put the fire out despite the horrible danger of being killed along with all on board. A crewman, moved by the captain's bravery, shouted after him, "Mr. Franklin, you're a brave man; you shan't go to hell alone."

The captain's courage and his success at putting the fire

out so inspired Rev. Bush that he challenged the Concord Lyceum, "Is it not by the courage always to do the right thing that the fires of hell shall be put out?" With these words, "Do the Right Thing" became the Bush family motto and has been passed from generation to generation.[7]

Rev. Bush continued his pastoral work first in San Francisco and then at Staten Island. His ministry seemed to be flourishing, yet a year later he resigned his pastorate. It was a crisis of theology that led to the break, and it had been long in coming. Some years before, a friend had quoted lines from Emerson's "Problem," a poem in which Emerson expressed his doubt about the clergy and his preference for a more naturalistic faith. James recognized Emerson's sentiments as his own, and this set him in tension with his orthodox Episcopal vows.

Rev. Bush wrestled with his conscience for years until even a friend could note, "He was by nature and constitution a Liberal, but did not know it, until his own moral nature had grown strong enough to break the shell of automatic habit."[8] When the shell finally broke, James resigned his post and moved to Concord, Massachusetts, where he lived the life of a latter-day Thoreau, delighting in nature and beloved by his neighbors, until his death in 1889.

There were also in the Bush line men of industry and civic vision. Of James' four surviving children, one seemed to have been possessed of that amazing combination of giftedness and grace that has a way of surfacing in some families. His name was Samuel, and he lived an astonishing life. He was a baseball and tennis star, sang with the finest of baritones, and was the vice president of the student body at Stevens College, where he majored in mechanical engineering. After graduation, he married a descendant of Robert R. Livingston, the Puritan dissenter who came to America in 1673.

Samuel became a leader in Ohio politics, ran a railroad, organized the first War Chest drive during World War I at the request of the famed financier Bernard Baruch, and founded the golf course that would become the training ground for Jack Nicklaus. He believed in civic duty, in giving back to the country that gave him a chance to succeed. The description we have of Samuel from William Barrett might well describe many of the men in the Bush line: "Mr. Bush was above the average, about six feet, rather slender in build, of graceful carriage. He had a fine, strong, handsome face, with a kindly smile and charming grace of manner. His chief characteristics, it seems to me, were a nature free from guile, and a gentle cordiality of manner refreshing to see. Pure and unspotted from the world, he was in the truest sense a spiritually minded man. Possessing strong opinions, he never was offensive or aggressive in asserting them."[9]

Clearly, Samuel Bush was an exceptional man of personal virtue and civic mission, son of a broadly spiritual man of literary and philosophical depth, who was in turn son of a boisterous adventurer and warrior. These are the men who bring us more directly to our story, for Samuel's son was Prescott Bush. We have already met him. He was the large man at the airstrip in Corpus Christi, Texas, the one who gave his twenty-year-old pilot-son the cuff links. He is the father of the first President Bush, the grandfather of George W. Bush, and he is the moral fire of the twentieth-century Bush family.

Prescott Bush was born on May 15, 1895, and in many ways he continued the pattern of the Bush men. He attended Yale like James Bush, could sing like Samuel Bush, and, when World War I began, he rushed off to serve in the Europe of General Pershing with a hunger for adventure that would have made old Obediah proud. After the war, he married a feisty beauty by the name of Dorothy at St. Anne's by the Sea, a small church in Kennebunkport, Maine.

Prescott went into business, prospered, and quickly earned a lifelong reputation for high character when he exposed a profit-skimming scheme that was draining his father-in-law's rubber company. His gifts landed him on Wall Street, where his success was legendary, and when World War II began, he was a powerful enough figure to be entrusted with the chairmanship of the USO (United Service Organizations). He gained nationwide recognition as he traveled the country raising millions for the National War Fund.

During his rise to fame, Prescott and Dorothy had four children. The first, Prescott Jr., was born in 1922. The second was George. He came into the world in 1924 in a Victorian house the Bushes owned on Adams Street in Milton, Massachusetts. One day it would be of more than passing interest that the street was named for John Quincy Adams, the son of the second president of the United States.

After the war, Prescott decided to run for the U.S. Senate. He failed twice but finally won as a Republican with Eisenhower and Nixon leading the ticket. He served in the Senate for a decade and was a prominent figure during the critical years of the late 1950s and early 1960s. Prescott cosponsored the establishment of the Peace Corps, funded the Polaris submarine project, and strongly supported civil rights legislation. He also favored a higher minimum wage and was a primary sponsor of the federal highway system. He was one of the men who helped make the Eisenhower years a transitional time in American history.

Yet, it was the moral fire of Prescott Bush that left its strongest impression on his sons and grandsons. Jeb Bush once described him as "a stern, righteous man."[10] He was. Friends called him a "Ten Commandments man." He insisted on ties and jackets at meals, expected his family to call him "Senator," and demanded athletic excellence of everyone—even his wife. Yet for all this rugged authoritarianism, it was his high moral sense and Christian faith that left the deepest mark.

One example is particularly important, not only for the ethical passion it reveals but also because Prescott's grandson was a witness, and the lesson never left him. It took place the summer of George W.'s junior year at Andover. Prescott had been invited to speak at the graduation of the Rosemary Hall girls' school in Greenwich, Connecticut. The audience certainly expected the usual senatorial graduation speech, but Prescott was in no mood for a polite little talk. He had been inflamed by the conduct of New York governor Nelson Rockefeller, who was running for president at the time. Rockefeller had divorced his wife of thirty-two years and married a recently divorced, much younger woman. Divorce under any circumstances was unusual for the time, but it was equally unusual for a U.S. senator to rebuke publicly a national figure at a commencement address. Prescott Bush spared Rockefeller nothing:

> Have we come to the point in our life as a nation where the governor of a great state—one who perhaps aspires to the nomination for president of the United States—can desert a good wife, mother of his grown children, divorce her, then persuade the mother of four youngsters to abandon her husband and their four children and marry the governor?...Have we come to the point where one of the two great political parties will confer upon such a one its highest honor and greatest responsibility? I venture to hope not.[11]

It was an astonishing moment, and George W. never forgot it. He was sitting in the audience as his senator-grandfather spoke, deeply moved by the older man's moral courage. The experience formed part of the foundation of his political philosophy. Years later, George W. would tell an interviewer, "I can remember my grandfather going after Nelson Rockefeller for his divorce…which at that point in politics was taboo.…There is a concept that you are responsible for your behavior. You can't shirk off your problems on somebody else. You must handle them yourself. There is the individual code of honor and respect for your neighbor. There is the religious undertone and a very strong religious sense for this. I guess what we have all inherited is the basis for political philosophy, if we're political people."[12]

And so the lessons were passed from generation to generation. Do the right thing. Strive for excellence. Give something back to the country. Do not shirk your responsibility. Be faithful to the religious sense. These lessons, captured in the note and the cuff links, are what George Bush, the father, meant to press into the heart of his governor-elect son on that January day in 1995.

—⁂—

It is not without significance that George W. Bush chose one of the hymns for that inaugural prayer service, the one he wept through with his father's note in hand. The hymn was a Methodist standard, one of Charles Wesley's best-known and one that George W. had come to love and make his own. It was called "A Charge to Keep I Have," and its background is worth noting. The words come almost without change from *Matthew Henry's Commentary on the Bible,* a Christian classic. They are drawn from Henry's reflections on Leviticus 8:35 where the temple priesthood is told to "keep the charge of the Lord." As Henry wrote:

> We have every one of us a charge to keep, an eternal God to glorify, an immortal soul to provide

for, needful duty to be done, our generation to serve; and it must be our daily care to keep this charge, for it is the charge of the Lord our Master, who will shortly call us to an account about it, and it is at our utmost peril if we neglect it. Keep it *that you die not;* it is death, eternal death, to betray the trust we are charged with; by the consideration of this we must be kept in awe.[13]

As Charles Wesley reflected on Henry's words, he formed them into one of his more than five hundred hymns. They became the lyrics to "A Charge to Keep I Have," which is so loved by many Methodists today that it is often sung at the close of denominational conferences as a call to change the world.

> A charge to keep I have,
> A God to glorify,
> A never-dying soul to save,
> And fit it for the sky.
>
> To serve the present age,
> My calling to fulfill:
> O may it all my powers engage
> To do my Master's will!
>
> Arm me with jealous care,
> As in Thy sight to live,
> And O Thy servant, Lord, prepare
> A strict account to give!
>
> Help me to watch and pray,
> And on Thyself rely,
> Assured, if I my trust betray,
> I shall for ever die.[14]

George W. Bush loved the hymn, alive as it was with a sense of duty and its powerful call to a destiny fulfilled, both familiar to him as family traits. He not only requested it be sung at his inauguration, but he also used its title as the title of his autobiography. Clearly, it is a theme of his life.

But Bush takes his charge with a twist. Not long after assuming his place in the Texas governor's mansion, Bush's longtime friends, Joe and Jan O'Neill, loaned him a painting. The governor was so moved by it that he had it placed directly opposite his desk so he could always have it in view while he worked. It is called *A Charge to Keep*.

That the painting and the hymn are linked in Bush's mind says a great deal about his view of calling, of destiny, and of leadership. The painting is by W. H. D. Koerner, a German immigrant who is often compared to Frederick Remington in his depictions of the American West. In the same tradition, *A Charge to Keep* shows a western rider spurring his horse up a difficult hill—alone.

After the painting was hung in the governor's office, Bush sent a memo to his staff. "I thought I would share with you," he wrote, "a recent bit of Texas history which epitomizes our mission. When you come into my office, please take a look at the beautiful painting of a horseman determinedly charging up what appears to be a steep and rough trail. This is us. What adds complete life to the painting for me is the message of Charles Wesley that we serve One greater than ourselves."[15]

It is the perfect picture for George W. Bush's vision of leadership, fashioned as it is by a legacy too powerful to ignore. He has taken the words of a Puritan, passed them through the lyrics of a Methodist hymn writer, and wrapped them in Texas boot leather to send them charging over a rugged hill in search of destiny. He has taken the Christian faith with all its depth and heritage, and he has incarnated them in the eternal symbol of the lone horseman. For him, it is the man who trusts God and charges over a daunting hill into the unknown who fashions history, who makes the world better for those who come after.

Faith. Courage. A valiant charge. A destiny to grasp. A legacy to fulfill. These are the themes of George W. Bush's life, his leadership, and his soul. And he sees them in play as he sees himself charging, in his mind's eye, over that imaginary hill in the Koerner painting. Bush is that horseman. His destiny is on the other side of that hill. God is with him, and no ruggedness of trail or modern version of a horse-mounted enemy will keep him from his duty.

He has *a charge to keep*. And now, in the Bush family line as in the nation, he believes it is "his turn."

Legacy of faith: The Bush family attends church in Houston, TX, 1964. L to R: Barbara, George, Jeb (hidden), Dorothy, Neil (looking at Dorothy), Marvin, George W.

CHAPTER TWO

And Manfully to Fight

It is a warm New Haven day in the summer of 1946. The congregation gathered in the quaint, cruciform church is just standing to hear the reading of God's Word. As they do, their minister moves to a spot behind the baptismal font and nods to a young family. The lanky husband steps to the aisle and allows his wife to go first, for she is tenderly cradling the baby boy who will now be pledged to the God of his parents.

The minister waits. He is a regal figure. His robes are the deep green that the Christian church has used for centuries to signify the latter months of Pentecost. His vestments match the altar cloth, the candles, even the bookmark in the large Bible on the altar. All are part of a grand drama celebrated by the faithful since that first Pentecost, when Christians believe the Spirit of Jesus descended upon 120 pioneers of their faith somewhere in Jerusalem.

"Hear the words of the Gospel," the minister says in practiced voice, the family and attendants now in place. *"They brought young children to Christ, that he should touch them: and his disciples rebuked those that brought them. But when Jesus saw it, he was much displeased, and said unto them, 'Suffer the little children to come unto me, and forbid them not: for of such is the kingdom of God.'"*[1]

So the liturgy from the *Book of Common Prayer* begins. Across the marble font from the minister stands the father. Tall, thin, and beaming, his name is George Herbert Walker Bush. On his face are all the conflicting emotions of first fatherhood: pride, tearful joy, apprehension, and hope. He is the son of Prescott Bush, the Wall Street legend and future United States senator, which means he has been trained to achieve and achieve gloriously. The drive to excel runs in his blood.

He has already achieved a great deal. A standout scholar/athlete at Andover, one of the nation's premier all-male prep schools, he held off entering Yale so he could join the Navy and fly torpedo bombers for his country. On September 2, 1944, he was shot down on a mission over the islands of Japan. After parachuting into the Pacific Ocean and floating for hours, he was rescued, miraculously, by an American submarine. For his bravery he was awarded the Distinguished Flying Cross. Returning home a war hero, George entered Yale, married his sweetheart, and became a star on his college baseball team. It is the summer of his sophomore year now as he stands to ask his God to redeem the soul of his son.

The question of his own soul, however, will one day become more a matter of debate than he would ever wish it to be. In the years ahead, a new force in American politics called the *Religious Right* will ask candidates for office to declare themselves publicly on spiritual matters. George will seek to make his mark in politics, and his clumsiness in discussing the deep things of the heart will not serve him well.

There is a word the Bush family uses often when speaking of emotions and religion. It is the word *personal*. It is at times used almost with resentment. Though they are public people, they believe deeply in privacy and despise the assumption that the deepest issues of their souls ought to be grist for the public mill. Their griefs, their faith, their intimacies, their innermost thoughts are just that: theirs. It is an assumption from a different time and of a different culture, but it is their assumption, one that will often put them at odds with an increasingly tell-all age.

George is clearly a man of faith. Raised an Episcopalian, he has absorbed an elegant form of Christianity from the aristocratic culture in which he lives: from the dinnertime preaching of his devout father, from the religious life of Andover, from the Episcopal parish life of his family. How deeply this faith embeds in his own soul early on is hard to say, particularly for him.

However, like Churchill on escape from a Boer prison camp in South Africa or Lincoln upon the death of his son, crisis confronted George with the eternal. It came as he was floating for those hours in the Pacific, unsure whether or not he was living his last moments on earth. "I was praying, crying out to God for help," he later said. "And then there was this calm, this sense of faith, that somehow I was going to live. It was not a sudden thing, a seeing of the light, but rather an inner peace."[2]

It was an experience that would sustain him through the years, but it did not satisfy those who demanded to know if he was "born again." The language confused him. His critics sensed it and doubted him. He tried to clarify: "If by 'born again' one is asking, 'Do you accept Jesus Christ as your personal Savior?' then I could answer a clear-cut *yes*. No hesitancy, no awkwardness." Had he left it there, he likely would have passed muster with the Religious Right. But he had to be honest. This language of the soul was new to him, and if he was going to attempt to speak it, he would have to tell the truth—all of it: "But if one is asking 'Has there been one single moment, above any others, in which your life has been instantly changed?', then I can't say this has happened, since there have been many moments."[3]

When he spoke in this way before a roomful of conservative Christians, the sense of letdown was palpable. It made matters worse when he tried to answer questions designed to draw him out. Renowned Presbyterian pastor Dr. D. James Kennedy had created a popular program for soul winning called "Evangelism Explosion," which was centered on the question "If you were to die tonight and God asked you why He should let you into His heaven, what would you say?" For evangelicals and fundamentalists, this was *the* question: What gets you into heaven? But rather than answering simply that he had trusted in Christ as his Redeemer, George would fumble and haltingly offer truisms about virtue, being a good man, and loving other people.

He was once asked what he thought about as he floated in the ocean for those desperate hours after being shot down near Japan. He answered, "Mom and Dad, about our country, about God...and about the separation of church and state."[4] It sounded to some like he was shoving every religious phrase he could remember into a single sentence. It did not wash with the Religious Right, particularly when they compared Bush with the warm and articulate Pat Robertson or the weepy Baptist governor from Little Rock named Bill Clinton.

Yet it was George Bush who, as his first presidential act, led the nation in prayer during his inauguration speech on January 20, 1989, and asked God to "make us strong to do Your work."[5] It was George Bush who was criticized for a friendship with Jerry Falwell but who refused to distance himself from the sometimes caustic fundamentalist. And it was when describing George Bush to his son George W. that the Rev. Robert Schuller said, "I never saw anyone pray like your father that day, and I don't think you did. It was a very deeply moving prayer."[6] He was recalling a visit to the White House in 1989. Terrorists in Lebanon had just executed a Marine officer and were threatening to kill other military hostages. The president was profoundly concerned, and Schuller never forgot the prayers he heard in the Oval Office that day.

It was also George Bush who could show a tender, searching side of his faith. He had lost a daughter, Robin, to leukemia. She was only three when she died. He was devastated: "I would slip into our church sometimes when no one was there. I would ask God, 'Why? Why this little innocent girl?'" It was a lonely, tortuous time, but he never forgot the lessons he learned in that valley. "I have never lost the faith and spiritual insight from that experience," he later said. "Actually, the pain of that experience taught us just how dependent on God we really are, and how important our faith is. In a moment like that, all you have is God."[7]

But all this is far in the future. George Herbert Walker Bush stands now not as world leader or embattled campaigner. He stands now simply as a father, facing the minister dressed in green before the font that holds the water that will cleanse the sins of his son. It is a warm summer day in New Haven. The year is 1946. George is offering his firstborn child to God, and all seems full of promise.

We call upon thee for this child, now to be baptized: of thy bounteous mercy, we beseech thee to receive him, grant unto him the forgiveness of his sins, and so fill him with thy Holy Spirit that he may grow in grace and godliness; and being steadfast in faith, joyful through hope, and rooted in love, may continue thine for ever; through Jesus Christ our Lord.

At George's side, holding the child, is Barbara. He calls her *Babs*. She is a direct descendant of the fourteenth president of the United States, Franklin Pierce, and daughter of the president of McCall Publishing Company. Born and raised in Rye, New York, she has lived the life of the well-born and well-bred: the finishing school, the doting servants, the Social Registry, the networking of the upper class.

Yet, there is something refreshingly down-to-earth about her. Perhaps it is that she is the third of four children and has had to be a little tougher than the rest. Perhaps it is that her relationship with her mother is not the best, and she leans to her brilliant, self-made, big-hearted father. Whatever the case, she is remarkably unpretentious given her background, yet never excessively earthy. She is poetic yet plain-spoken, almost eager to cut a few inches from the self-important and the proud but adept at inspiring the low.

And she is fearless. Shortly after her wedding, George's father came upon her as she was having a quiet smoke. "That's not a nice habit for a woman," he growled, while lighting a cigar. She did not flinch. "I smoked before I became your daughter-in-law," she fired back, "so you can't lecture me now."[8] It did not matter to her that he was her father-in-law and one of the most powerful men in the America. She was right. That's all that mattered.

This bluntness will remain with her throughout her life and will not lift in matters of religion. She has been raised a Presbyterian and, like her husband, has a deep faith but cannot point to a single transforming moment. Her faith has come Presbyterian-style: through a process, a wooing, a repeated cycle of seed time and harvest. She cherishes it. It is deep, personal—not for public display. She is suspicious of flaunted spirituality.

When her husband is president, she will have to play hostess to some of the leading television preachers of the day. It is not always a pleasant experience. "I'm offended when they think they are the ones who discovered God," she will write in her diary. "He has played such an important part in our lives." She is put off by pride and pomposity. Anyone appearing arrogantly holy is a candidate for a shot across their bow. When Jimmy Swaggart visited the Bushes in the White House, he declared that anyone who likes country music is immoral. "That does *me* in," the leader of the free world replied.[9]

The mixture of religion and politics is sometimes confusing, often hurtful to her. When Pat Robertson defeated her husband in the Iowa primary, the host of *The 700 Club* announced to the world that "God deserves credit for the victory." Naturally, this was offensive to the wife of the defeated candidate. "God is important in our lives, too," she retorted. "It's just more personal."[10] What is striking here is both her use of the word *personal* and the assumption that Pat Robertson's public faith is not as personal as the Bushes'. She does not intend judgment. The statement reveals her lifetime assumption that the more public something is the less a matter of the heart it is. This is, again, a different culture and value system speaking, but the day will come when the faith of her own son will challenge her thinking.

And she will have more to do with that son's faith than many would think. It is she who will make sure that the family regularly attends church. It is she who will guarantee that Billy Graham is a frequent guest in the home. She is the one who will quietly ask friends to pray for the salvation of her children. In many ways, she is the vital spiritual influence in her family. When a noted Christian musician visits the Bush White House, his conclusion will be, "George is a Christian, but Barbara is a believer."

The service is nearing an end. George and Barbara stand side by side before the minister dressed in green. The man of God is asking them a question.

Do ye solemnly believe all the Articles of the Christian Faith, as contained in the Apostles' Creed; and do ye acknowledge the obligation, as far as in you lies, to provide that this child be brought up in the nurture and admonition of the Lord, that he be diligently instructed in the Holy Scriptures, and he be taught the Creed, the Lord's Prayer, the Ten Commandments, and all other things which a Christian ought to know and believe to his soul's health?

There is no hesitation. They knew the question was coming and have reflected upon it in the earnest manner unique to first-time parents. "We do," they reply together.

O Merciful God, grant that the old Adam in this child may be so buried, that the new man may be raised up in him.

Grant that all sinful affections may die in him, and that all things belonging to the Spirit may live and grow in him.

Grant that he may have power and strength to have victory, and triumph against the devil, the world, and the flesh.

And the minister gently takes the child from the mother, pours water over him, and proclaims:

George Walker Bush, I baptize thee in the Name of the Father, and of the Son, and of the Holy Ghost.

Barbara receives the child again from the minister, who then lifts his voice to proclaim:

We receive this child into the congregation of Christ's Flock; and pray that hereafter he shall not be ashamed to confess the faith of Christ crucified; but manfully fight under his banner, against sin, the world, and the devil; and continue Christ's faithful soldier and servant unto his life's end. Amen. [11]

—⁂—

George W. Bush was born in the first year of the post–World War II period, the first year of what came to be known as the baby-boom era in America and a year in which the newspaper headlines were eerily prophetic of what the remaining half of the century would be like.

In March of that year, Winston Churchill told the world that a Communist "iron curtain" was descending across Europe. A month later, a British-American committee called for the partition of Palestine into independent Arab and Jewish states. In July, Mother Frances Xavier Cabrini became the first U.S. citizen to be canonized by the Roman Catholic Church. That same month, the United States began atomic tests at Bikini Atoll in the Marshall Islands. In a strange connection of history, models on the fashion runways of Paris were soon sporting the first bikini bathing suits. More ominously, in November, French forces bombed Haiphong in Vietnam, killing more than six thousand Vietnamese and signaling the first futile attempts to maintain control of French Indochina.

Headlines for literature and the arts were equally symbolic of what was to come. It was in 1946 that Dr. Benjamin Spock published *The Commonsense Book of Baby and Child Care* and so launched the parenting revolution that would shape a generation. Irving Berlin's score for *Annie Get Your*

Gun was all the rage, its most memorable tunes reading like themes for the century: "There's No Business Like Show Business," "Doin' What Comes Naturally," and "Anything You Can Do (I Can Do Better)." *The Best Years of Our Lives* was the year's most popular film and swept the Oscars. Eugene O'Neill published *The Iceman Cometh,* Alfred Hitchcock directed *Notorious,* and Simone de Beauvoir offered an Existentialist view of death in *All Men Are Mortal.* It was a year of contrasts before a half century of confusion.

World politics and the arts aside, what would most shape America starting that year was the astonishing level of prosperity she was about to enjoy. The United States owned 90 percent of the world's gold, had emerged triumphant from sixteen years of depression and war, and had undergone a technological revolution during the war years that was just beginning to show up in consumer goods. America was rich and about to get richer. Suburbs, highways, sleek cars, shiny kitchen appliances, college, leisure time, children, television, the business of America being business—these would soon become the preoccupations of most Americans and of the returning GIs, in particular.

That George W. Bush was born in 1946 does much to explain the man he would become. He is a study in contrasts, a composite of cultural materials one rarely sees combined. In this he is, in part, a product of his age, for he is a baby boomer with an upper-class twist. Like many of his generation, he has partied hard, surfed the sensual/spiritual spectrum, and become more gently conservative in his latter years. He has pulled away from his parents only to return and find himself wondering if he will ever be as good as the "greatest generation" was. He is eclectic, restless, and intuitive, as we will see. He and his generation have changed jobs, changed dwellings, and changed dreams more than any other in American history. They have given us pet rocks and the PC, the frivolous and the ingenious. They are the most creative, unsettled, inconsistent, brilliant, and self-ishly compassionate generation on earth. And he is of their tribe.

And yet he also falls outside some of the stereotypes of his generation. He seems less imprisoned by the destructive narcissism of his time. He is not very introspective and does not seem to be caught in the cycle of extremes that dizzy many in his generation. He seems simpler, less easily impressed, more energetic, and a bit more respectful than his peers. And he has seldom veered far from his mooring in family, faith, and a sometimes too simple political philosophy.

He does not quite fit the pattern of his time, and historians will long wonder at the mystery. They will search hard for the sources of his uniqueness and will hopefully tell us more as the years go by. But if they truly want the answers, they should begin where he says the story begins—on the barren, windswept stage of West Texas.

—⁂—

He came into the world uncharacteristically late. His impatient grandmother was unwilling to tolerate his delay and finally insisted that his mother drink castor oil. All resistance ended, the baby came, and Barbara's only disappointment was that the child did not weigh every bit of the sixty pounds she had gained during the pregnancy. He was apparently an expressive child from the beginning. Barbara's mother said she hated leaving his range of sight because the child always looked hurt that he was no longer the center of attention. The future politician was already "working the room."

It is noteworthy that even in his first year of life he was often taken to a baseball field. Not only did he watch his father play first base as the captain of the Yale team, but young George W. was adopted by the school's groundskeeper Morris Greenberg, who would often take the boy to work and let him play on the diamond. Sometimes he took him to the Peabody Museum, and it is here that George W. Bush's "life of crime" began. Mr. Greenberg showed the wide-eyed child the skeleton of a huge dinosaur housed at the museum. George W. was amazed and could not wait to go home and tell his mother. As he excitedly recounted his adventure, he proudly handed his mother a paper bag. She looked inside and found bones her son had taken from the dinosaur's tail. The bones were quickly returned—without any hint of a cover-up.

George W. remembers none of this, though, because his first memories are of Midland, Texas. In 1948, his father graduated from Yale with a degree in economics and set out for West Texas the very next day. He had decided not to follow Prescott Bush to Wall Street but rather to make his own way. "I wanted to do something on my own," he later said. "I did not want to be in the shadow of this very powerful and respected man."[12] It is a telling statement. Clearly, George H. W. Bush wanted to break free of his button-down New England life with its staid conventions and throw himself into the risky, promising world of oil town West Texas. Perhaps he wanted to test himself in a profession his father had not prepared for him. Or perhaps it was simply that there was big money to be made. Whatever the reason, his decision to move to Midland in 1948 would forever change his son's life.

"I don't know what percentage of me is Midland," George W. Bush once said, "but I would say people—if they want to understand me—need to understand Midland and the attitude of Midland."[13] It is not uncommon for a youth to have absorbed so deeply the values of a place that his heart later returns there even when his body cannot. Some transaction has occurred, some impartation. The memories become infused with a meaning, a kind of emotional archaeology, that reinforces, that inspires, and that sometimes protects. Midland is that place for George W. Bush. While governor of Texas, he was having a conversation with an associate when he suddenly blurted out, "If I died today, I'd like to be buried in Midland."[14] He was not making funeral plans. He was locating his heart.

Midland and her sister city, Odessa, became the capitals of a miniature oil nation when the Santa Rita No. 1 oil well blew in May of 1923. The map showed the place as Reagan County. Catholic investors had jokingly suggested that the well should be named for Rita, the saint of the impossible. The Santa Rita well defied its name and drew to sleepy towns of the petroleum-rich Permian Basin the oil-thirsty from around the world.

West Texas is a flat, treeless, dusty, hardscrabble land. Visitors from the east are often astonished by how large the sky seems. There are no mountains or trees to block the view, and they are tempted to call West Texas "Big Sky Country," much to the consternation of folks in Montana who rightly lay claim to the description. What passes for a tree is in fact a weed called mesquite, and tumbleweeds are so large and plentiful that some West Texans used to paint them for Christmas. Buildings are often one story and flat roofed. Rock gardens are common, often with a cactus as the centerpiece. Walls are adorned with family portraits, proudly killed animals, and other emblems of a West Texas memory: barbed wire, cow skins, rope knots, paintings of cowboys, and Western landscapes.

The oil industry by nature draws together tribes that do not normally mix. There are the wealthy and not-so-wealthy investors, the highly educated engineers and geologists, the drillers, the roughnecks, the roustabouts, the accountants and bankers, the truckers, the warehouse foremen, the yard bosses, the ever-present lawyers, and dozens of attendant services: restaurants, hotels, barbecue pits, mechanics, bars, prostitutes, equipment stores, dance halls, truck salesmen, bookies, insurance agents, and maybe a church or two.

Midland became a place of overlapping cultures. There were first the authentic Midlanders. With a heritage of railroads and cattle ranching, the citizens of Midland were a gracious, hardworking, religious people. Children always addressed their elders formally, and a man of fifty-five would refer to a man of sixty as "Mr." and "Sir." Doors were normally left unlocked, and nothing was worse in this communal world than a bad reputation. Conversation was highly prized, and men gathered against trucks, under trees, and on porches to trade stories and lore. Women did the same with toddlers at their feet. Midlanders were a friendly, newsy, down-home people. Outsiders were treated with caution but respect.

When news of oil in West Texas reached the world, the authentic Midlanders were invaded. There was the moneyed Ivy League crowd from the East with soft palms, a bookish understanding of the world, and just enough arrogance to "make a man wanna take a shot at the boy." There were also the roughnecks and laborers—white, Mexican, and a few blacks—who worked hard, drank hard, fought hard, broke things up, got arrested, and started it all over again. There were also trainloads of visitors who ranged from Eastern investors, to members of the press, to government regulators looking for something to tax or control.

What emerged in time was a new kind of man. We see

Hollywood's attempt to capture him in George Stevens' 1956 film *Giant*, based on Edna Ferber's novel and starring Rock Hudson, Elizabeth Taylor, and James Dean in the last performance of his life. Whatever its failings, the film captures the merging of cattle culture and oil culture, Eastern ways transplanted onto Western barrenness, and how wealth deforms. There was a new culture rising, and the language began to reflect the new reality. When a woman was asked what her father did for a living—he was pointed out in business suit, boots, cowboy hat, saddlebag briefcase, and climbing into a limousine—she said simply, "He's an oil rancher."

—◆—

This was the budding culture that met two-year-old George W. Bush and his mother when they stepped onto the tarmac of the Odessa airstrip in 1948. It had to be a shock for Barbara. The home her husband found for her was a duplex along an unpaved road with prostitutes living next door. One shooed away farm animals to get to the outhouse. The stench could be overwhelming. One night Barbara awoke in a panic and rushed the family out of the house. She had smelled gas and thought they were in danger. Neighbors explained that the wind was simply carrying fumes from the nearby petroleum plants.

Barbara had to change. Her husband was already changing. The Ivy League war hero and star athlete worked like a common day laborer and rubbed shoulders with men who did not know where Connecticut was. He sold oil field equipment, learned the business from the ground up, and sometimes overdid his enjoyments. One Christmas Eve, his firm celebrated with an open bar, and George, who did not drink much, probably did not want to be a standout teetotaler.

Barbara knew he was home when a pickup truck roared through the front yard, threw out a bundle, and drove off. The bundle was her drunken husband. The man hears about it to this day.

Those who write of the Bush family in Midland will be tempted to emphasize what a change from the East that West Texas was for them. This is true of the parents, but not of the son. For George W., Midland was home, normal, the world as it should be. It is not hard to see the manly energy of Midland embedding itself in his system. Midland tripled in size during the decade the Bush family lived there. From an overwhelmed cow town it became a mini-metropolis of skyscrapers rising from scrub brush and cactus. The competitive Bush DNA meant George W.'s father met with success and took the family through a series of ever-nicer homes, symbolic of an ever-increasing prosperity. George W. lived from the age of two until the age of twelve in a forward-looking, achievement-oriented, back-slapping, competitive, loud, hard-drinking, big-eating, hard-playing culture. And he thrived on it.

His preschool years were almost idyllic, complete with doting parents, rowdy bike adventures, explorations of the local creek or buffalo wallow, and Buck Rogers or cowboy movies at the Ritz Theatre. He quickly learned that baseball was the key to his father's pride and the respect of his friends. His dad taught him the game and how the game is a metaphor for life. One of his happiest moments came when his baseball star father told him he no longer had to hold back when playing catch. He could throw full speed because he knew George W. could handle it. The words felt like a welcome to manhood.

He attended Sam Houston Elementary and was a raucous and popular student. Sadly, he would always associate the school with the death of his sister. Robin had contracted one of the most dreaded of childhood diseases—leukemia—and would battle it for seven excruciating months. George and Barbara kept the knowledge of how bad it was from their children. George W. was only seven, and they did not want to burden him. He knew only that Robin was sick and doctors were tending her in New York. Then one day he saw his parent's car pulling into the school parking lot and was sure he saw his sister in the back seat. They had brought her home, he thought, and he could not wait to see her. He joyously ran to the car only to hear his tearful parents say that she would not be coming home—ever. Robin was dead.

A depression settled on the Bush home. The pain became physical and kept George and Barbara up at night. Decades later, the memory of her death could still cut them. Nothing would ever be the same. The mood in the home had an unusual effect on little George W. He began to feel that it was his job to cheer his parents up. He started telling stories and jokes, anything to see a smile again on his mother's grieving face. One day Barbara overheard her son telling a neighbor child that he could not play because his mother needed him. "That started my cure," she wrote in her best-selling memoirs. "I realized I was too much of a burden for a little seven-year-old boy to carry."[15]

This story reveals something important about his personality. Even at seven years of age, he felt he had the power to make those around him *feel* differently. Call it charm or personality, wit or a winsome manner, he believed he had a force within him that could lift spirits and restore. It says much about how he saw himself and about how his life in Midland gave him a chance to explore his effect on an ever-widening assortment of people.

He attended San Jacinto Junior High, ran for president of

his seventh-grade class and won. He got straight As, starred in football and baseball, and was known as a popular kid with a big mouth. He was arrogant, aggressive, fast, and sarcastic. But he did not mind showing tenderness. Once when the mother driving the cheerleaders to a football game got lost and the cheerleading squad was missing for much of the game, George W. noticed. When the girls arrived, he told them he'd been worried and asked if they were OK. In the world of West Texas football, cheerleaders are eye candy to be ignored during the game by any self-respecting player. George W. was breaking code, but he did not care. It seems that compassion could at times overcome cool.

His world was cowboy as much as it was transplanted Yale. He knew men who shined their boots for church and left their pistol belt in their truck to go inside for dinner. He knew of deadly knife fights, the "kill-it and-grill-it" ethos of the Western outdoorsman, and he knew to make noise in the scrub brush to keep the rattlesnakes away. He was no transplant to the world of cowboy hats, boots, big silver buckles, rifles, horses, and roping. It was part of the only world he knew.

He also knew sports, and in the way that shapes character rather than entertains a crowd. His father coached his baseball team and amazed the young boys with his skills. They all wanted to be like him, George W. most of all. This is what sports will do: give a man a model. It is not insignificant that he was the quarterback of his football team in a town with legendary rivalries. George W. learned sports as the controlled combat of the principled, and the lessons learned never left him.

Whether he knew it or not, he was absorbing a sense of what it meant to be a man. He knew the violent and the hard and the ruggedly skilled. He also knew manhood as the force that makes a family whole, a woman safe, a child confident, and a community strong. He had watched his father treat his mother well, serve in church, coach with character, yet command respect in the bruisingly masculine world of the oil patch. He knew the earthy and the off-color, as well. It is all-important, for though he will have his playboy years, he will eventually allow a Midland brand of manhood to merge with a resolute faith. It will form a tempered aggression, and it will serve his principles well. People will find it refreshing in a world of uncertain genders.

We should not ignore the Bush family's involvement in Midland's First Presbyterian Church. We know his dad served on committees and raised funds, his mom could not have escaped baking something or teaching the children, and young George W. certainly sat through Sunday school classes and played out his personality before the church youth group.

The fact is, though, that church was part of their lives only as a strand in the fabric of Midland life. This is not to question their personal faith—though it is doubtful that George W. had one at this point—but rather to question the role of the church in that faith during these years. The truth is that Midland was their church, as it were, and not exclusively the building they entered on Sunday morning. This is why Midland plays such a major role in George W. Bush's thinking today.

The Midland of his memory is not far from the Midland of reality, but when he speaks of it, he sounds as if he's describing a scene from *It's a Wonderful Life.* It is hard for our cynical culture to take him seriously. What is important is not that his memory completely fits reality—though it is close—but that the Midland of memory is the core image of his life, his West Texas version of a New Jerusalem. Listen:

Midland was a small town, with small-town values. We learned to respect our elders, to do what they said, and to be good neighbors. We went to church. Families spent time together, outside, the grown-ups talking with neighbors while the kids played ball or with marbles and yo-yos. Our homework and schoolwork were important. The town's leading citizens worked hard to attract the best teachers to our schools. No one locked their doors, because you could trust your friends and neighbors. It was a happy childhood. I was surrounded by love and friends and sports.[16]

There is much for the hardened to scoff at in this. Yet for those who want insight into George W. Bush, they will find its greatest source here. What this man thinks he knew in Midland is what he believes life on earth ought to be. Whether he idealizes it or not is far from the question. The important point is that his experience in Midland, filtered by time though it may be, is his ideal, the way he believes human beings should live everywhere.

We can take the point further. When he finds true faith later in his life, his conversion illuminates much of what he has already absorbed in Midland. It makes him a better man. And it frames his world-view. In a sense, he invades Iraq— yes, to root out a terrorist threat and remove Saddam—but to make it a Midland of the Middle East; not so much as an exact cultural and industrial parallel but as the model of how human beings ought to live together. His hopes for a post-war Iraq are safety, family, benevolent political leaders, good schools, sports, friends, and love. All men should live this way, he believes. It is what he wants America to be and for America to model in the world.

Religion is more than what happens in a church, a temple, a synagogue, or a mosque. It is that externalized value system that makes culture what it is. It is the way of things, the ultimate concerns of a people. The point here is not that George W. Bush's faith is some kind of mystical Midland to be imposed upon the world. The point is that if we are going to know a man's faith, we must follow what he believes outside of religious institutions and categories to where it makes itself known in the streets. For Bush, those beliefs carry both us and him to the decade he spent as a boy in Midland and to the authentic living he saw there. It is why he is able to say that Midland is who he is.

—m—

George W. began to understand just how rooted in the soil of Midland he was when the Bush family moved to Houston. The wealth, elitism, and callousness they encountered in the Lone Star State's biggest city must have felt familiar to his parents. They had known it in the East. But for George W. it was a colder, lonelier world. He failed to get into St. John's, the best private school in Houston, and ended up in the less rigorous but still prestigious Kinkaid. His classmates were beyond him. Once he was waiting for the school bus when a friend offered him a ride. The boy was no more than fourteen and was driving his own sports car. He definitely was not in Midland anymore. In time, he would make friends, thrive in sports, and get top marks in school, but he had been fitted for Midland. Houston was a foreign land.

His sense of dislocation may have cracked the door of his heart to matters of faith. He served as an altar boy at St. Martin's Episcopal Church where his family attended, and he was drawn to the sensuality of the liturgy: "I loved the formality, the ritual, the candles and there, I felt the first stirrings of a faith that would be years in the shaping."[17]

These words are not those of a fourteen-year-old, of course, but rather of a fifty-year-old reflecting on his life. Like his parents, he will never be able to point to a transforming moment, an instantaneous spiritual awakening. He knows that he has not come to faith suddenly, but that faith has arisen in him over the years. It will wax and wane, and there will be times when some will wonder if his life will be a promise unfulfilled. But the day will come when all of the faith that has been planted in him—from childhood prayers to Presbyterian creeds, from small-town Christian culture to the Christ known in an Episcopal service—will flower to become the ruling principle of his life. But it is the desert he will know before this flowering that will make it all the sweeter when it comes.

Ivy League fun: George W. Bush during his years at
Yale University, 1964–1968.

CHAPTER THREE

The Nomadic Years

When a man becomes president of the United States, it is hard to view his prior life as anything other than a predetermined course to the White House. Unless we see the man apart from his office, though, we cannot really see the man, and for few presidents has this been more the case than for George W. Bush.

It is easy to see the Bush story in terms of inevitabilities. He was the first son of a president of the United States. He was wealthy, handsome, and personable. He had degrees from two of the best universities in the world. Yet by the time Bush turned forty, many considered him a failure. He had fallen woefully short of his father's achievements at the same age, had lived a largely aimless life, and had failed at almost every venture he started.

What is more, he was notoriously inarticulate and drank so heavily he once challenged his own father to a fistfight.

Astonishingly, twelve years later this same man would be the Republican frontrunner for president of the United States. It is a fact that demands understanding both of the years Bush himself called "nomadic" as well as the transformation that brought his aimlessness to an end and empowered him to achieve.

—⚍—

In the fall of 1961, George W. Bush followed in his father's footsteps and entered the esteemed Phillips Academy, Andover. With tradition reaching back to the American Revolution, the school boasted former students as diverse as Oliver Wendell Holmes and Humphrey Bogart.

A *Time* magazine article from 1962 described Andover as the best prep school in the nation but also expressed concerns. Some thought the school too busy, too academic, and too focused on placing graduates in the Ivy League. Among the critics was former English department chairman Emory Basford: "The spirit of man is neglected in this school. These boys admire managerial things. Even when they collect clothes for the poor, it is done as a study in organization. A little boy likes to linger, to look at bugs and birds. Here he has to hurry away because he hasn't time. This has become a strange, bewildering, killing place." As though to make the point, the principal of a smaller school sent one of his boys to spend a week at Andover. The young man lived in the dorm, went to classes, and played chess—"and nobody knew he was there."[1]

George W. Bush used two words to describe the place: "damp" and "dark."[2] The regimented lifestyle, the formal dress code, and the mandatory chapel services five days a week were almost more than he could endure. It was, he said later, "a hard transition." The truth is that he was lonely. When time allowed for making friends, though, he settled in. His two nicknames at Andover reveal much about him at the time. His friends called him "Lip" because of his insolence and "Tweed" because he started a stickball league and ruled it like the famous Boss Tweed of Tammany Hall a century before. When he did not qualify for the varsity sports teams, he became a cheerleader. The Andover yearbook for the time includes a photograph labeled "Bush and his gang." It was a theme of his life: the gregarious, handsome, wise-cracking Texan, never the top student or athlete but always the energetic heart of the crowd.

As he settled into his schoolwork, he encountered a problem that has possibly plagued him all his life. He was given an assignment to write about a strong personal emotion, and he chose his grief at the death of his sister, Robin. Deciding that the word *tears* was too unsophisticated for Andover, he used a thesaurus his mother had given him and chose as a substitute the word *lacerates*. Obviously, he had chosen the wrong sense of *tears*. The teacher returned the paper with a zero and the words "Disgraceful: See me immediately." Bush turned to his friends and said, "How am I going to last a week?"[3]

The story touches on a theme that Gail Sheehy has developed in an article for *Vanity Fair*. Sheehy raises the possibility that George W. is an undiagnosed dyslexic and cites a dyslexia specialist on the incident at Andover: "It suggests he really didn't understand the language," that he could not "distinguish between the word 'tears,' meaning to rip, and 'tears,' meaning crying." The expert continued by saying, "Bush is probably dyslexic, although he has probably never been diagnosed."[4]

Sheehy's thesis would explain a great deal. Dyslexia is not a matter of intelligence, but it does run in families and does lead to the kind of linguistic confusion Bush will be known for all his life. Sheehy cites an expert in the diagnoses of dyslexia: "Dyslexics hear adequately but seem unable to process quickly all the sounds in the word. So when they go to retrieve a word they've heard, they will sometimes omit sounds, or transpose or even substitute sounds. They are highly verbal. But a language-disordered person is not particularly organized as a speaker."[5]

Bush will become famous for just this kind of linguistic confusion—what *Harper's Magazine* referred to as "Dubya as a Second Language." "Tactical [nuclear] weapons" is condensed into "tacular weapon," "enthralling" becomes "inebriating," and "handcuffs" is transformed into "cuff links."[6] Speaking of John McCain, Bush once told a group of reporters, "The senator...can't have it both ways. He can't take the high horse and then claim the low road."[7]

Dyslexics who operate in the public eye tend to overcome their verbal gaffs by becoming actors, meaning that they emphasize connecting with the audience in nonverbal ways and with short, memorized scripts that make the chances of a blurted inanity less likely. They are personable, make quick studies of people, and often master the body language and quips that draw people in. Sheehy's description of Bush working a room is typical: "He violates the normal social distance and moves right in, four or five inches from the stranger's mouth or eyes, and he drinks in the face. He seems to be memorizing visual cues—modeling the person in his mind's eye the way a sculptor would. If this is his compensation for an unreliable verbal channel, it works, and particularly for a politician it works wonderfully."[8]

That Bush might be dyslexic makes his academic struggles and successes all the more poignant.[9] In this he is not unlike his hero, Winston Churchill. In his school years,

Churchill was always at the bottom of his class, a great embarrassment to his parents. There is evidence to suggest that Churchill was also dyslexic: his poor reading skills early in life, his need to rehearse thoroughly every speech for fear of losing his thought, and his notoriously short attention span.

Later in life, Churchill thought he knew what hindered him: "Where my reason, imagination, or interest were not engaged, I would not or I could not learn."[10] Perhaps for the dyslexic to learn he must have his imagination stimulated. In Churchill's case, this stimulation came through an early English teacher and his own program of self-education. For Bush, it came through the legendary Andover history teacher Tom Lyons.

Bush has said repeatedly that Tom Lyons "was probably the most influential teacher on me."[11] Yet Bush was as moved by the man as he was by his teaching. Lyons had been a promising scholar and athlete at Brown University in 1954 when doctors discovered he had polio. His athletic career cruelly ended, he finished a degree in history and a master's in teaching at Harvard before joining the faculty at Mount Hermon School in western Massachusetts. He sustained his love of sports by coaching. All their lives players remembered the image of Coach Lyons excitedly swinging down the sidelines on his crutches. In 1963, he accepted a teaching post at Andover, drawn primarily by the excellent history faculty there. Over the next thirty-six years, he would become one of the school's heroes, the kind of teacher who made students tremble and alumni proud.

Lyons was a powerfully built man with silver hair and a rich, full voice. His students remembered his intensity and passion, how he would storm his classroom. One alumnus recalled, "He stands up and he's waving those long silver crutches, and banging them on the table. You didn't dare fall asleep. And he knew everything. He would wander around, smacking the table, smacking you and getting you to think. It was the most exciting class I've ever taken."[12]

Lyons's passion was American history. His courses were a combination of fiery lectures, original sources, and carefully orchestrated discussion. "You ask a question here," Lyons recounted excitedly, gesturing to an empty classroom, "the student responds, then *this kid* makes a comment. *This kid* challenges, and *this kid* chimes in. You say something, then *this kid* over here and it starts again. That takes a lot of preparation. It's way easier to give a lecture or just ask Socratic questions."[13]

The son of a reporter for the *Boston Globe*, Lyons cared passionately about the human side of history. His philosophy for understanding the past was an interplay of events, ideas, and the people who shape them. He spoke in terms of heroes but understood mass movements. He specialized in the history of the Supreme Court and the Civil Rights movement. To one tearful student he said, "Don't worry, I'm trying to push you. You have to get the human element. I don't want to read two pages with statistics and bureaucratic stuff. Find people who are interesting, and tell the story through them."[14]

Lyons came to Andover during George W.'s senior year. He coached the young man in football and taught him American history. He remembers Bush as an "enthusiastic kid," "a boy of spirit," and "all for winning." "Given the student body of the time, he was in the middle," Lyons recalls, "but this is the middle of a class that had the same SAT scores as the entering class at Harvard. He was not the student his father was, and no one would have thought he would grow up to be president. I would remember him even if he had not become president, though, for his spirit."[15]

The romance of the past as Tom Lyons re-created it had a deep impact on George W. "He taught me that history brings the past and its lessons to life," Bush later wrote, "and those lessons can often help predict the future. Tom Lyons's descriptions of events that shaped America's political history captured my imagination. Not only was he a great teacher, but also he was an inspiring man."[16] When Bush left Andover for Yale in 1964, history was both his inspiration and his intended major.

Because he had found Andover "cold and distant and difficult," George W. determined to make a better start at Yale.[17] He memorized the names of his classmates in the Yale student registry and roamed the campus in search of friends. He joined a fraternity, coasted academically, and when his skills failed him on the freshman baseball team, he played rugby—largely for the after-game party. He fared better at Yale than he had at Andover, but he still lacked purpose. Nothing revealed this quite like his decision to get engaged.

He had met Cathryn Wolfman in Houston and dated her long distance during his early years at Yale. He proposed over the Christmas break of his junior year. His friends were astonished. It was odd for a junior to decide to marry with his senior year still ahead. Besides, no one seemed more the bachelor playboy than Bush. Yet just as his family and friends were getting used to the idea, the engagement ended. The Houston press began reporting that Bush broke up with Wolfman because she was Jewish. But Wolfman was an Episcopalian. The engagement ended for other reasons.

According to Lacey Neuhaus, a friend who knew both Bush and Wolfman during their college years, the engagement fizzled out because Wolfman set off on her life's direction while Bush remained aimless and unsure. "I don't think he'd figured out what he liked about himself yet," said

Neuhaus, "or what he liked about life, except for baseball."[18] When Bush visited Wolfman in Washington, it became obvious that she had purpose he lacked, and the relationship dissolved soon thereafter.

This lack of an inner fire plagued Bush for some time. It may have been one of the reasons he was so eager to enter Skull and Bones, a secret society at Yale. Designed for "converting the idle progeny of the ruling class into morally serious leaders of the establishment," Skull and Bones accepted fifteen seniors each year with the goal of making them "Good Men," known as "Bonies," a play on the French word for "good."[19] The club reportedly began in a break with the Phi Beta Kappa honor society over the issue of secrecy. The dissidents met in a chapel adorned with skull and crossbones, which gave them both their name and their emblem. That they met in a building called "the Tomb" only added to their mystique.

Myths have long surrounded the society, including that they brand their members, that they pledge themselves to one world government, and that they secretly study the black arts. Conspiracy theorists abound, and there are websites that claim to have "exposed" Bush's involvement. However, as Helen Thorpe has written for *Texas Monthly*, "The truth is rather mundane: It's a club of fifteen students who meet regularly to learn more about each other."[20] What Skull and Bones probably did for Bush, other than providing him with a moneyed old boy network, was to expose him to Bonies of vastly different backgrounds. Among fellow members in his day were men like Donald Etra, an Orthodox Jew, and Muhammad Saleh, a Jordanian Arab.

Bush's mention of the society in his book, *A Charge to Keep*, has not served him well. He writes, "My senior year I joined Skull and Bones, a secret society, so secret I can't say anything more."[21] It is hard to imagine a sentence better designed to awaken suspicion. He should have known better. During his vice presidential campaign, the senior Bush was compelled to resign his membership in the Trilateral Commission when errant suspicions arose that he served the political agenda of the Council on Foreign Relations in pursuit of a "New World Order." George W. had already fielded dozens of questions about such matters both as a candidate himself and in his father's campaigns. He could have handled the matter more wisely. Still, though the Skull and Bones legacy would haunt both Bushes throughout their careers, the network it gave them opened important doors.

—⁂—

When Bush graduated from Yale in 1968, he was eager to get back to Texas. He had grown weary of "snobs" and "intellectual arrogance."[22] He missed the warmth of his home state. Typical of the experiences that had turned him off at Yale was a talk he had with the campus chaplain, the liberal activist William Sloane Coffin. It took place just after Bush's father was defeated in a race for the Senate by Ralph Yarborough, the incumbent Democrat. Friends had seen the younger Bush weeping alone the night his father lost. Sometime afterward, George W. saw Coffin on campus and introduced himself. The chaplain, whose assignment was to comfort the students and guide their spiritual development, replied, "Yeah, I know your father, and your father lost to a better man."[23] The words stung Bush, and he remembers them to this day as one of the reasons he hastened himself back to Texas: "Texas people are more polite. I don't think a Texan would do that to a son."[24] It would be memories like these that would keep Bush from attending a Yale reunion for decades.

Returning to Houston, Bush continued to live as a man without meaning. He later wrote of these years, "I had not yet settled on a path in life."[25] It was an understatement. His years at Andover and Yale revealed a man capable of great imagination, someone gifted for leadership, yet who was clearly uninspired. He had no sense of destiny and seemed unwilling to invest in anything that failed to hold his fascination. And nothing but history in the hands of Tom Lyons and the thrill of sports really had thus far. To put it simply, he was bored: not in the sense that he had nothing to do but rather in the sense that he had found nothing worth doing.

He drove around Houston in his Triumph, dated beautiful women—including the daughter of designer Oleg Cassini—and learned to fly jets for the Texas Air National Guard at nearby Ellington Air Force Base. He listlessly worked a variety of jobs: on an offshore oil rig, for an agri-business firm, in a program for inner-city youth. By all accounts, he did none of them well or for long. His energies were reserved for women, parties, and boisterous games of water volleyball at the Chateaux Dijon apartments where he lived.

There has long been heated speculation about Bush's immorality during this time. Did the future president use drugs? Did he have sex? Did he get drunk? Did he use foul language? Did he look at pornography? The questions seem naïve. The likelihood is that he did it all. The mystery is that anyone is surprised.

Bush was at the time a wealthy, good-looking, Ivy League graduate during the moral revolution of the late sixties and early seventies. He had a trickle of Christianity running through his life, but it was far from a controlling current. He lived the life of the world as it was, and in time, he would find it wanting and change course. He has refused to detail his "so-called wild, exotic days," because he will not "play the game" with reporters.[26] The truth of the matter has probably been captured best by Howard Fineman, who in his *Newsweek* article "Bush and God" quipped, "Come-to-Jesus stories are more dramatic if the sinner is a pro. Bush was a semipro."[27]

The embarrassing end of this period is marked by a disturbing confrontation. During a visit with his parents in Washington, George W. went out drinking with his younger brother, Marvin, who was only fifteen. As the two drove back to their parent's house, they ran over a neighbor's trash can. Father Bush demanded an explanation, to which the inebriated young George W. snapped, "You want to go *mano a mano* right here?" It was Jeb Bush who rescued the moment, and probably his brother, by announcing that W. had secretly applied to and been accepted to Harvard Business School. The family was stunned, and the senior Bush said, "You should think about that, son." "Oh, I'm not going," the younger man replied testily. "I just wanted to let you know I could get in."[28]

The truth was that George W. had also applied to the University of Texas Law School and been rejected. The rejection did not sit well with his competitive soul, but friends had told him he would be better off elsewhere. Many fresh lawyers out of U.T. were finding it hard to land the top-paying jobs. Bush had also heard that business school demanded analysis more than theorizing and literary skill. That suited him perfectly. Besides, he had no other plan. "I wasn't really that excited about going," he said, and added, "I think if you look at my full life…I haven't had a game plan."[29] He was still drifting, but he decided that a Harvard drift was better than a Houston party drift.

Bush remembers that the taxi driver dropped him off at Harvard Business School and said, "Here you are at the West

Point of capitalism."[30] The reality was that Harvard in those days was moving further and further away from West Point. These were the Watergate years, and the consensus on campus was that Richard Nixon, the man who had given George W.'s father his last two jobs, had to go. Bush would remember hearing speakers like Muhammad Ali, John Kenneth Galbraith, and Dick Gregory, who told his audience on Class Day that young whites were "America's new niggers."[31]

Though Bush was a bit more serious as a student than he had been at Yale, he still found time to maintain his reputation as the king of camaraderie. He joined old friends from Andover and Yale who were also at Harvard and found the only place in Boston at the time where a man could hear a George Jones record: a bar called the Hillbilly Ranch. Bush would don his flight jacket, put his can of Skoal chewing tobacco in its appropriate pocket, and dart off to down the closest thing to a Lone Star longneck he could find.

He remembers that Harvard "gave me the tools and the vocabulary of the business world. It taught me the principles of capital, how it is accumulated, risked, spent, and managed."[32] It also taught him where the money was. While he was at Harvard, the business school released a study showing that the highest-paying jobs were to be found in petroleum and research. Armed with this information and his memories of Midland, he decided to head back to Texas where yet another oil boom was under way. Just after graduation, he drove his 1970 Cutlass along virtually the same route his father had taken in 1948, both of them seeking to make their fortunes in the oil-rich Permian Basin of West Texas.

—⁂—

Years later he said he was happy when he returned to Midland because he was answering "the entrepreneurial call

I felt in my soul."[33] The Ivy Leaguer started out in a $100-a-day job searching through courthouse records. It was a living, but he had bigger dreams. He used connections and a trust fund to acquire leases for potential ventures of his own and soon formed an exploration company called Arbusto Energy (pronounced *ar-boos-to*, the Spanish word for "bush"). But when the firm drilled several dry holes, friends called it "Arbusted."

The conventional wisdom was that you "raise your hell in Odessa and your family in Midland." Bush spent a lot of time in Odessa. During the day he traded on his father's business connections and loyalties, and at night he traded stories over bourbon and beer. In 1976, while vacationing at the family home in Kennebunkport, Maine, he was stopped by local police after a night of partying. He was charged with DUI, and his Maine driver's license was suspended for a month.[34] It was not his finest hour. His father called to thank the police for their care. Before long the matter was all but forgotten by everyone concerned. The humiliation and the drinking, however, remained.[35]

In 1977, Bush was reintroduced to Laura Welch on a date set up by family friend Joe O'Neill. George W. and Laura had been classmates at Sam Houston Elementary School and had even been neighbors at the Chateaux Dijon in Houston. They met now as though for the first time and quickly fell in love. Three months later, they married.

That Laura was a civilizing if not quite a settling influence in George W.'s life is certain. She was a gentle Texas lady, the reader he never was, and a methodical public school librarian who knew how to bring order to chaos. Friends had called his Midland apartment "the toxic waste dump." Perhaps Laura's greatest influence on him, though, was in drawing him to her Methodist church.

He found it suited him better, as he explained years later: "The Episcopal Church is very ritualistic, and it has a kind of repetition to the service. It's the same service, basically, over and over again. Different sermon, of course. The Methodist Church is lower key. We don't have the kneeling. And I'm sure there is some kind of heavy doctrinal difference as well, which I'm not sophisticated enough to explain to you."[36] His change of church was typical of his brand of decision-making: relational, practical, nonintrospective, and defined in the simplest terms.

Though George W. and Laura honeymooned in Mexico, the family joke is that the new couple's extended honeymoon was a campaign for Congress. At the age of thirty-one, Bush decided to run for the Nineteenth Congressional District seat against a Democratic state senator named Kent Hance. It was a campaign marred by inexperience. Bush filmed a commercial that showed him jogging, a pursuit cowboys and oilmen took as an "eastern college boy thang." He allowed Hance to paint as sinister the campaign contributions he was receiving from New York and even to paint his excellent education as a negative. He also allowed his opponent, in a move that anticipated the tactics of the as yet unformed Religious Right, to claim the moral high ground. These were lessons he would never forget.

The lessons began for Bush when he discovered that citizens of his district were receiving a letter from Hance addressing them as "Dear Fellow Christians." In the letter, Hance attacked Bush for an ad his campaign had taken out in the Texas Tech student newspaper promising free beer at a Bush rally. Five days later, Bush lost to Hance, 53 to 47 percent.

Bush says the ad promising the free beer ran without his knowledge two months before Hance's letter went out. More importantly, Bush knew that Hance owned property on which a Lubbock bar, a place popular with the Tech students called "Fat Dogs," was located. The vice chair of the Republican Party in Lubbock, Ruth Schiermeyer, begged Bush to use the information as a counter to Hance's charges. Bush refused: "Ruthie, Kent Hance is not a bad person, and I'm not going to destroy him in his hometown. This is not an issue. If I try to destroy him to win, I don't win."[37] Nevertheless, Hance continued talking about how the alcohol issue showed the difference in the backgrounds of the two candidates. The tactic worked and swayed a good many votes. It was a harsh introduction to how religion and politics could mix, and Bush would remember it well in the years to come.

Despite his disappointment with the election, George W. returned to his struggling company, continued to seek investors, and continued to drill mostly dry holes. Though his personal wealth increased, largely through investments and spotty income from Arbusto, his company never thrived. Finally, as Bush approached forty, the bottom fell out. Midland became ground zero for one of the biggest financial busts in history, culminating in the collapse of the First National Bank in 1983, with over $1.2 billion in assets and twelve hundred employees.

—⁂—

We should freeze this moment in Bush's life, for it is of enormous significance. He is, on the one hand, the son of a respected national leader, the graduate of esteemed universities, nearly a millionaire, and the owner of an oil company. He's a pillar in the local Methodist church, a faithful husband, and an adoring parent by this time, the father of twins.

Yet, he is, in many ways, a failure. Even if one were to ignore for the moment his obvious problem with alcohol, he is, as his cousin John Ellis has said, "on the road to nowhere at forty."[38] Ellis believes the crisis was one of comparison: "You have to really understand how much his father was loved and respected by so many people to understand what it would be like to grow up as a namesake, the son of George Bush. These are the parallels in his life. He went to Andover, went to Yale, went to West Texas, ran for Congress, and at every stage of that he was found wanting. To go through every stage of life and be found wanting and know that people find you wanting, that's a real grind."

The burden might have crushed him. Men have committed suicide over less, ruined marriages and children in their attempts at self-rescue. But before long something would change in Bush, and it would give him the direction his life had lacked. In Ellis's words, "He gathered it together." Though he was "going nowhere at forty...At the age of 52, he's the front-runner for the Republican presidential nomination. That's a pretty incredible turnaround."[39]

Spiritual guidance: George W. and Laura Bush with Billy and Franklin Graham in Jacksonville, Florida, November 5, 2000.

CHAPTER FOUR

Of Men and Mustard Seeds

Men come to faith in many ways. Some have single dramatic experiences that fill them with certainty. Some cling to their parents' God from childhood and never depart. Others live through gut-wrenching cycles of doubt and belief until the latter triumphs. Still others arrive at faith through a process of years—layer upon layer, as though a temple of the heart is being readied for a destined moment. This is how faith came for George W. Bush.

By the time he passed his fortieth birthday, Bush had been churched and churched thoroughly. He was baptized in a New Haven Episcopal church, trained for a decade in the First Presbyterian Church of Midland, and made to feel "stirrings of faith" in St. Martin's Episcopal Church of Houston. During his Andover years, he was required to be in a Congregationalist-style chapel five times a week, which meant he spent as much time in church in those three years as a normal attender does in ten. Once he got to Yale, he began taking religion in small doses. Perhaps he needed a break.

It was Laura who drew him in again and made him a Methodist. Not long after their marriage, he was teaching Sunday school at First Methodist in Midland, taking up offerings, and sitting on committees. It was the manner of most of his life. Whether his heart was engaged by it or not, he had known since childhood that a good man stays connected to his faith, that he does his duty in the house of his God. And so he did. A friend once remarked that if Bush had stopped going to church at the age of forty, he would still have attended more than most people do in a lifetime.

But, again, he was bored. And when he was bored, he joked.

Laura took him to a James Dobson seminar in hopes of seeing him deepen spiritually. It did not take. George W. got up from his seat and moved next to a friend. The quips began. "What kind of pants did the Levites wear?" he whispered.

Another time, a pastor asked, "What is a prophet?" Bush sang out, "That is when revenues exceed expenditures. No one's seen that out here in years." On another occasion a teacher startled a daydreaming George W. by asking, "What happened to the Jew on his way to Jericho?" After a brief silence, he responded, "He got his butt whipped."

He relished being the bad boy. He once set the timer on his watch to go off in the middle of a talk by a Sunday school teacher who was notoriously long-winded. The chuckles were hard to suppress, and the next week the hapless teacher was met by a chorus of chirping watches.[1] It was juvenile, typical of the bored and the unengaged.

By 1984, though, events conspired to help him concentrate. World oil prices started collapsing, and the slide would continue until crude dropped below $10 a barrel, down from a high of $37. Life in Midland changed dramatically. The big-spending came to a neck-snapping halt, and the town in which one of every forty-five citizens had been a millionaire began to see foreclosure, bankruptcy, and fear. Bush's small firm lost more than $400,000, and there were more hits to come.

The economy was but one force driving Bush into confrontation with himself. He had a list of failures and an unrelenting sense that he had fallen short of his famous name. To top it all, he had never shaken his chief demon: the aimlessness, the lack of purpose, the boredom that had plagued him all his life. He had no sense of destiny, at least not one that came from the heart. He could party and do business and love his family, but he did not have the inner fire that makes men happy and great. He was a lightweight in almost every sense, and he seemed to know it and set out in search of answers.

The story of Bush's spiritual transformation has usually centered upon his famous walk on a Maine beach with Billy Graham. Bush has said that Graham "planted a mustard seed in my soul," but if this is so, it happened only after a year of deep plowing by others.[2]

In 1984, the spiritual leaders of Midland were trying to tend the souls of a troubled community. As Bush later wrote, "Midland was hurting. A lot of people were looking for comfort and strength and direction."[3] To bring the needed healing, the city's churches invited the people of the region to gather at the Chaparral Center in the first week of April to hear famed evangelist Arthur Blessitt. Beginning in 1969, Blessitt had achieved world renown when he began carrying a cross on long walks while he preached. He had said he intended to carry the cross around the world, for he believed Jesus had personally commanded him to "carry the cross on foot...identify My message in the highways, road-sides where the people are."[4]

By 2002, Blessitt had carried the 12-foot cross over 38,800 miles in 284 nations. The *Guinness Book of World Records* lists Blessitt's effort as "The World's Longest Walk."[5] During his journeys, the evangelist shared his message with the common people he met in the streets as well as world leaders like Pope John Paul II, Muammar Qaddafi, Yasser Arafat and Boutros Boutros-Ghali, the former Secretary General to the United Nations. In 1972, Billy Graham had joined Blessitt in war-torn Ireland to walk the streets of Belfast and pray for the peace of the city. The cross-carrying evangelist seemed to be everywhere and was quickly becoming one of the best-known religious leaders in the country.

Billed as "Decision '84," Blessitt's meetings in Midland were widely advertised on radio and television. Handbills and posters invited Midlanders to attend "with the sincere prayer that we might experience the grace of the Lord Jesus Christ, and the fellowship of the Spirit." There was a growing sense of excitement in the city. Blessitt had spoken in 1982 at Midland's First Baptist Church, and his reputation for leaving changed lives in his wake now only heightened expectations.

The meetings began on the first of April. Every evening, Blessitt preached to the thousands who jammed the Chaparral Center. He sometimes found himself talking to seekers of every kind until the wee hours of the morning: oilmen, high school students, even discouraged ministers. During the day, Blessitt carried the cross around Midland, spoke in school assemblies, and talked with almost anyone willing to engage him on the streets.

Something special seemed to be happening. Blessitt remembers that there was a "particularly strong spirit of renewal" in Midland. People were amazed at the hundreds who made commitments to Jesus in the meetings each night, and they were even more astonished when fifty people answered a special invitation to commit their lives to full-time ministry. Blessitt sensed the holiness of what was happening. He told the organizers of the meetings that he would not take money for appearing, that he had "decided not to take a cent" from the economically troubled community. It was a surprising move, rare among traveling evangelists. Some strongly urged Blessitt to reconsider, but he refused—and his determination only added to the wonder of what was happening.[6]

On April 3, several days into the meetings, Blessitt received a call from Jim Sale, an oilman, Baptist Church member, and one of the organizers of the crusade. Sale told Blessitt that there was another local oilman who had heard the radio advertising and wanted to meet him. But this was no ordinary oilman, Sale explained. This was George W. Bush, the son of the vice president of the United States. Blessitt agreed to see him, and the three met that day in the coffee shop of Midland's Holiday Inn.

Blessitt and Sale both recount the exchange that followed: After a brief greeting, Bush looked at Blessitt and said, "Arthur, I did not feel comfortable attending the meeting, but I want to talk to you about how to know Jesus Christ and how to follow Him."[7]

The evangelist reflected for a moment and asked, "What is your relationship with Jesus?"

"I'm not sure," Bush replied.

"Let me ask you this question," Blessitt probed. "If you died this moment, do you have the assurance you would go to heaven?"

Bush did not hesitate. "No," he answered.

The evangelist then began to explain what it meant to know and follow Jesus. He quoted Scripture after Scripture, commenting as he went, and making application to Bush's life. After he had outlined the Christian message, he said, "The call of Jesus is for us to repent and believe. The choice is like this. Would you rather live with Jesus in your life, or live without Him?"

"With Him," Bush replied.

"Jesus changes us from the inside out," Blessitt continued. "The world tries to change us from the outside in. Jesus is not condemning you. He wants to save you and cleanse your heart and change your desires. He wants to write your name in the Book of Life and welcome you into His family, now and forever." Blessitt then asked Jim Sale to tell of his own changed life, believing that Bush would relate to the testimony of a fellow oilman.

When Sale was done, Blessitt said, "Mr. Bush, I would like to pray a prayer for you, and then lead you in a prayer of commitment and salvation. You can become a follower of Jesus now."

Bush had some questions, though, and the two men took time to answer each one until he seemed satisfied.

The evangelist pressed again: "I want to pray with you now."

"I'd like that," Bush said.

Blessitt then prayed, asking Bush to repeat each phrase after him. The evangelist remembers the prayer as follows.

—∞—

Dear God, I believe in You, and I need You in my life. Have mercy on me a sinner. Lord Jesus, as best as I know how, I want to follow You. Cleanse me from my sins, and come into my life as my Savior

and Lord. I believe You lived without sin, died on the cross for my
sins, and arose again on the third day, and have now ascended
unto the Father. I love You, Lord; take control of my life. I believe
You hear my prayer. I welcome the Holy Spirit of God to lead me
in Your way. I forgive everyone, and I ask You to fill me with Your
Holy Spirit and give me love for all people. Lead me to care for the
needs of others. Make my home in heaven, and write my name in
Your book in heaven. I accept the Lord Jesus Christ as my Savior
and desire to be a true believer in and follower of Jesus. Thank You,
God, for hearing my prayer. In Jesus' name I pray.[8]

When the prayer ended, Bush was smiling, and Blessitt
began "rejoicing." It was "an awesome and glorious
moment," the evangelist recalls. He read Luke 15:10 to Bush:
"There is joy in the presence of the angels of God over one
sinner who repents." Blessitt then gave Bush a pamphlet
called "The New Life," which explained how to grow as a
young Christian. After a few more pleasantries, the two
shook hands and parted. Over the following two years, they
spoke by phone several times, but eventually Blessitt's long
seasons of travel abroad caused them to lose contact.

Sale and Blessitt kept silent about the meeting for seventeen years, agreeing that it would not be proper to speak
publicly about the details of Bush's spiritual life. But when *A*
Charge to Keep was published in 2001, with Bush writing so
strongly about his faith, Blessitt decided that the time for
secrecy had passed. He published his recollection on his website and has often spoken of the prayer with Bush in his sermons. Jim Sale, the only other eyewitness, confirms that
"what happened is precisely as recorded in Blessitt's testimony." Indeed, Sale adds that given the seventeen years
Blessitt went without "saying a word, there is real humility

and integrity here that bears witness to the authenticity of the testimony."[9]

That Bush has never spoken publicly of the meeting is not surprising. For him it was but one in a series of events during that time that pressed the message he had known since childhood even more deeply into his heart. More revealing is how intensely Bush was searching out matters of the spirit. He obviously felt so uncomfortable with evangelistic meetings that he could not bring himself to attend the one in Midland. Yet he was so moved by what he heard Blessitt say on the radio that he sought a meeting with the man to ask him how to follow Jesus. Clearly, Bush was hungry for something he had yet to find in all of his religious experience. Just as clearly, though, the meeting with Blessitt did not bring Bush's search to an end. When Billy Graham asked him a year later if he was right with God, he answered, "No."[10]

If Bush was hungry, the conversion of his friend Don Jones, the president of Midland's fastest growing bank, was about to make him hungrier. Bush knew Jones well. He was on the board of Jones' bank, the two often drank together—Jones liked to joke that he was "raised Episcopalian, and where you find four Episcopalians, you'll usually find a fifth"—and they attended First Methodist Church together. For Jones the Episcopalian, the choice of a Methodist church was a compromise with his Southern Baptist wife.

Not unlike his friends at the time, Jones had a low opinion of the "born-again" variety of Christians. He thought of them in terms of flashy televangelists with overdone jewelry and sideshow-man suits. "I sure didn't want to be one," he laughs. A sense of moral neediness and some of the spiritual happenings in Midland led Jones in 1985 to make a New Year's resolution: give up drinking and start reading the

Bible. It was while home alone on the tenth of January that he was reading the Gospel of John and came upon the words, "Unless a man is born again, he shall not see the kingdom of God." Immediately, "an overwhelming sense of conviction and need for God's grace" came over him. There were tears and a crushing sense of his sinfulness. He prayed and cried and prayed some more. By evening, he felt peace, a sense that "the burden of his sins had been lifted from his soul." His wife came home to find a different man.[11]

Jones developed a deep love for the Bible, reading it "morning, noon, and night." He got even more involved in his church, and that November he started attending Community Bible Study, the Midland branch of a Bible study movement started in Washington, D.C. His transformation was immediately evident to everyone who knew him, including Bush. Jones gave his testimony wherever he had opportunity, and soon much of Midland knew that the prominent banker had been "born again." That Jones was a respected businessman and had such a pleasant way of talking about his faith made him easy for men like George W. Bush to relate to.[12]

It was just as Bush and his friends were marveling at Jones' transformation that the famous walk on the beach with Graham took place. In the summer of 1985, the Bush clan vacationed together at Kennebunkport, Maine. Graham joined them for a weekend and preached at the small summer church, St. Anne's by the Sea. Bush remembers that "one evening my dad asked Billy to answer questions from a big group of family gathered for the weekend. He sat by the fire and talked. And what he said sparked a change in my heart. I don't remember the exact words. It was more the power of his example. The Lord was so clearly reflected in his gentle and loving demeanor."[13]

As Bush reminisced with one reporter, "It was this beautiful Maine night and Billy just sat there and talked to us, and we asked him questions and shared our thoughts. He and I had a visit afterward—it was just a real personal religious visit—and I started reading the Bible."[14] The "visit afterward" was a walk that Graham and Bush took at Walker's Point the next day. During the conversation, Graham turned to Bush and said, "Are you right with God?" "No," Bush replied, "but I want to be."[15]

His response seems odd at first. He had been, in some loose sense, a Christian all his life. Just the year before, he had prayed with Arthur Blessitt to become a more devoted disciple. Yet, with Graham he found himself unable to say he was "right with God." Perhaps Bush compared himself with Don Jones and knew he had not experienced the same degree of transformation. Or perhaps just being with Graham issued a deeper challenge to his soul than he had yet known.

It is typical of Bush that he remembers how he felt to be with Graham rather than much of what he said. "I knew I was in the presence of a great man," he recalled in *A Charge to Keep*. "He was like a magnet; I felt drawn to seek something different. He didn't lecture or admonish; he shared warmth and concern. Billy Graham didn't make you feel guilty; he made you feel loved."[16]

The weekend changed him. It was both a culmination of events—his family heritage of faith, the years of churches and chapels, the prayer with Blessitt, the example of Jones— and the gentle plowing of his soul by a loving man of God. "Reverend Graham planted a mustard seed in my soul," Bush later wrote of those few days, "a seed that grew over the next year. I had always been a religious person, had regularly attended church, even taught Sunday school and served as an altar boy. But that weekend my faith took on new meaning. It was the beginning of a new walk where I would recommit my heart to Jesus Christ. I was humbled to learn that God sent His Son to die for a sinner like me."[17] He must have shared something of his experience with his family because sometime later he overheard his mother, Barbara, talking to someone on the phone. "I've got some exciting news," she said. "George has been born again."[18]

—m—

When he returned to Midland, he had a new hunger for the Scriptures. His friend Don Evans gave him a devotional Bible with daily readings from both Testaments, Psalms and Proverbs organized for every day of the year. "My interest in reading the Bible grew stronger and stronger," he remembers, "and the words became clearer and more meaningful."[19] He also joined the Community Bible Study that Don Jones attended. The group had begun meeting the year before around the time of the Blessitt meetings. By the time Bush joined, in fall of 1985, almost 120 men were gathering to study the New Testament writings of Luke.

It is possible Bush did not fully understand the enormity of what he had joined. The Community Bible Study (CBS) ministry began in 1975 with a group of women who wanted to see "effective" Bible studies serving the Washington, D.C., area. The class began at Fourth Presbyterian Church in Bethesda, Maryland, with over five hundred women gathering to study the Gospel of John. The leader was Lee Campbell, who had been deeply influenced in her faith by Christian theologian/historian Francis Schaeffer. The curriculum involved a systematic, verse-by-verse study of each book of the Bible. Students were required to work several hours outside of class, answering questions, meditating on the verses, and even turning the words to prayer.

The CBS movement began to spread quickly. Within four years, there were classes in ten states and London, England. Eventually, there were nineteen classes in the D.C. area alone. But it was not just its growth that distinguished CBS; it was influence. Early participants included Jack Kemp's wife, Joanne; Jim Baker's wife, Donna; Elizabeth Dole; and other key players in the "Reagan Revolution" of the eighties. Though nonpolitical and nondenominational, CBS often provided the biblical content that educational programs of local churches lacked.

This was certainly the case for Bush, who found himself now challenged to explore Scripture in a way he never had before. Every week Don Jones would drive Bush to the Bible study and marvel at his growth. Bush was still good for a laugh. Salvation did not entail a lobotomy or a personality bypass. Bush would always be a cutup. But it was not long before the men around him noticed a difference. The truths he was learning and pressing into his heart through prayer and meditation were clearly changing him. There was a new gravity, a new seriousness. George the Lightweight was being replaced by some other, as yet unknown being. Bruce Robertson, the leader of the Bible study, told the *Washington Post* about first noticing the difference in Bush: "Suddenly we were standing there talking very seriously about our spiritual life, and I remember thinking, 'Man, you've changed.'"[20]

The degree of change in Bush during this time raises the question of what, specifically, he was learning. "Just the Bible," according to Jim Tanner, a Dallas businessman who enrolled in CBS at about the same time as Bush. "We worked inductively through the entire Gospel of Luke. We focused on the life and work of Christ in such a way that dogmas and doctrines receded to the background while the sheer power of the story came alive. Basically, we were able to clear away all the centuries of religious trappings to see Jesus as He actually was."[21]

Seeing Jesus so vividly made Bush want to be a better man. Christian theology teaches that while salvation is instantaneous, sanctification—the process of cleaning up a believer's thinking and conduct—takes time. For Bush, a man of habit and routine, the moral renewing of his life presented a challenge. "It was like a long struggle up a steep hill for George," Don Jones has said.[22] It would take years for some habits to go. His tendency to strong language, for example, would die hard. Yet, his famed struggle with alcohol ended quickly, and it says much about the man he was becoming.

—⚬—

Bush has joked that he is so cheap he only stopped drinking because he saw the bar bill. The truth is that his moral compass and sense of values were being reconfigured by his deepening faith. He knew of Don Jones' decision to stop drinking and the good that it had done in his life. Still, getting drunk was the sin, not drinking alcohol, and he saw no reason to stop completely.

The change in his thinking came just after his fortieth birthday. The Bushes joined their friends the O'Neills and the Evanses for a trip to the Broadmoor Hotel in Colorado Springs. Long the retreat of kings and presidents, the Broadmoor is a beautiful estate nestled in the mountains near Pikes Peak and with all that a man might need to rest, recreate, and celebrate life. One evening, Bush celebrated as he usually did: by drinking. He had never consumed alcohol to slip into the comforting ooze of drunkenness. Like many extroverts, he drank because he thought it extended him: "Drinking…magnified aspects of my personality that probably don't need to be larger than they already are—made me more funny, more charming (I thought), more irrepressible. Also, according to my wife, somewhat boring and repetitive. What may have been funny in moderation was not so funny in exaggeration."[23]

Years of experience had taught him that running would help reset his system. After the night of drinking at the Broadmoor, he went for a run, assuming exercise would have its usual effect. It did not. "For the past fourteen years, I had run at least three miles almost every day. This run was different. I felt worse than usual, and about halfway through, I decided I would drink no more. I came back to the hotel room and told Laura I was through."[24]

He also told O'Neill, who was such a heavy drinker himself that he spoke openly of checking himself into the Betty Ford Clinic. O'Neill understood the social and health reasons for quitting but sensed Bush had something else on his mind, as well: "He looked in the mirror and said, 'Someday, I might embarrass my father. It might get my dad in trouble.' And boy, that was it. That's how high a priority it was. And he never took another drink."[25]

The decision to quit alcohol is a major turning point in Bush's life. At first it reveals what he was beginning to understand about his health, his marriage, and his family's reputation. But the ability to follow through on his commitment also reveals the kind of man that faith was making him. Whether he quit initially because he found it something he could not control or so as not to embarrass his father, the all-important point is that he found the discipline to serve a cause greater than himself. He made a major, life-changing move based on something that heretofore had been lacking in his life: purpose.

He had been ticketed for drunkenness, and it had not stopped him. His wife had asked him to quit, and he had not.

He had even made a fool of himself socially on more than one occasion.[26] That had not worked either. But once he came to faith, once he came to believe that his life was about a Jesus who died for him, he found both the purpose and the discipline to do something that nothing else in his life could induce him to do: sacrifice pleasure on the altar of a greater cause. This new discipline, fueled by a growing sense of purpose, was beginning to make him an exceptional man.

It is also important to note the way Bush stopped drinking. The *New York Times* said he did it in "a characteristic way: decisively, impulsively and without much evident introspection."[27] This would increasingly become a feature of both his personal life and his brand of leadership. Once he recovered his inner moral compass and understood its signals, he obeyed it by doing what he thought was "the right thing." He did not believe in "psychobabble" and "navel gazing." He believed in action. He just needed to know in which direction to act. Once his faith began to point the way, the gap between thought and action narrowed.

Certainly, he was flawed and would at times choose unwisely. Still, Bush the aimless, Bush the nomad, Bush the man without purpose was passing from the scene. In time—and it would take arduous steps over the course of years—he would become Bush the man with a charge to keep. Yet never would he forget what he might have been. Years later, when he had ascended to the presidency, he asked some religious leaders to pray for him by saying, "You know, I had a drinking problem. Right now I should be in a bar in Texas, not the Oval Office. There is only one reason that I am in the Oval Office and not in a bar. I found faith. I found God. I am here because of the power of prayer."[28]

For the love of the game: America's first fan throws out the first pitch at New York's Yankee Stadium, October 30, 2001.

CHAPTER FIVE

"My Faith Frees Me"

Whenen a man comes to faith for the first time, or when he scales greater heights in the faith he already has, he needs time apart from his routine. His soul yearns for some place nearly monastic where he can wash himself in the fresh fountains of his new beliefs. He needs time: time to bring his mind in step with his heart, time to see the world as though for the first time in the light of his new experience. Not too surprisingly, George W. Bush did not have such a season aside after his rebirth of faith, and this explains much about the kind of Christian he became in later years.

It was the summer of 1985 when Bush took his famous walk on a Maine beach with Billy Graham. By fall of that year, he was digging into the Bible with the men of the Community Bible Study. We might wish for him quiet years in Midland to explore his faith and deepen his relationship with his God. It was not to be.

In a matter of months, he was engineering the biggest oil deal of his life. That was in 1986, the year he stopped drinking. Late in that year, his father drew him into the presidential campaign that would dominate his life for the next eighteen months. While the confetti was still being swept up from his father's inauguration, he began taking ownership of the Texas Rangers and soon after started building one of the best ballparks in baseball. Scarcely two years later, he was campaigning to become the next governor of Texas.

A wise spiritual guide would have chosen a quieter season for him. Bush was not new to Christianity, but he did need time for the "mustard seeds" that Graham had planted to germinate. Not allowed such luxury, he grew spiritually on the run. He absorbed rather than studied. Drawing from the spiritual lives of those around him, he oriented to simple truths, personal experience, and stories. It served him well and had its benefits. Friends have noted that he is uncharacteristically teachable in spiritual matters.

But this hit-and-miss approach also left an unevenness in his spiritual life. He was inconsistently discipled, and it showed. He could help his father articulate a tender Christian faith in the morning and in the afternoon cuss out a journalist with language that would make a sailor blush. His mother said he now knew the Bible better than anyone in the family. Yet when famed spiritual leader James Robison met him during this time, Bush impressed him as mostly fun-seeking and sports-crazed. And this was in 1992, nearly seven years after Bush's conversion.

Nevertheless, these years cannot be dismissed as being without spiritual importance. They are critical to an understanding of how Bush's faith was changing him and inspiring him to achieve. The discerning can find in these years an unleashing of his energies, an impartation of some force that infused the former nomad with drive, with an intense hunger to make his mark.

In *A Charge to Keep*, he wrote, "My faith frees me. Frees me to put the problem of the moment in proper perspective. Frees me to make decisions that others might not like. Frees me to try to do the right thing, even though it may not poll well. Frees me to enjoy life and not worry about what comes next."[1] Such candid remarks offer a telling reflection. Another man might say his faith set healthy boundaries or pulled him from the pit or helped him to love or showed him who his Maker is. Bush had come to faith as an adult, almost in midlife, and, among all else that his faith did for him, it liberated him to be who he really was. His faith gave him the genuine version of what he wanted when he drank. He thought alcohol gave him George W. Bush made grand. It was not so. But faith gave him George W. Bush free to live as large as his God allowed.

—⁂—

A friend of the Bush family once said that George W. got religion, and to reward him God delivered him from the oil business. Whether true or not, some thought they could see the grace of God extended to Bush's business in 1986.

The company first called Arbusto had become the "Arebusted" of so many jokes that Bush finally changed the name to Bush Exploration Company. That operation had not done well, either. By 1983, it ranked 993 in terms of oil production in Texas. One of the investors sighed, "It was disastrous, through no fault of George's. The good Lord just didn't put any oil out there."[2] By 1984, when the oil world imploded, Bush's firm had merged with a company called Spectrum 7.

The firm was owned by two Cincinnati investors, William O. DeWitt Jr., a Yale alumnus, and Mercer Reynolds. This consortium also did poorly, and by 1986 its survival was in doubt.

Later that year, Dallas-based Harken Energy initiated efforts to buy Spectrum 7. As a business move, the purchase was a gamble. Some insiders wondered if Harken was not more interested in the Bush name than in the company. Paul Rea, Spectrum 7's geologist, told the *Washington Post*, "Having him with the company would be an asset...having George's name there. They wanted him on their board."[3] When the sale was complete, Bush ended up with "a sweetheart deal." Harken hired him at a salary of $120,000 a year and gave him $530,380 worth of stock.

There would always be questions about Bush's association with Harken. Not long after the purchase of Spectrum 7 and the hiring of Bush, Harken won a lucrative contract to drill for oil in Bahrain, in the Persian Gulf. But Harken had little experience in overseas exploration, and industry watchers suspected Bush's political connections made the deal possible. In 1990, Bush unloaded most of his stock, earning him $848,560 just two months before Harken posted a loss of more than $20 million. SEC investigations found no wrongdoing—but the SEC chairman was a former aide to George W.'s father. Critics, perhaps understandably, have never let the matter die.[4]

The deal with Harken freed Bush to respond to his father's call to arms. With the Reagan years winding to a close, the race for the White House was on. Reagan's vice president intended to extend his boss's legacy, and he wanted his sons, George W. and Jeb, at his side as he ran. George W. moved his family to a house on Washington's Massachusetts Avenue and went to work.

His father had told him, "You don't need a title. Everyone will know who you are." He was right: They knew *who* he was, but they did not know *what* he was. They were left with first impressions, and many drew the same conclusion James Robison had: young, untested, pleasure-seeking, and undefined. Bush aide Janet Mullins once said, "I remember thinking when I met George W. in 1987 that he could have gone either way: in the words of Lee Atwater, chump or champ."[5]

He cut a strange figure among the D.C. elite. Staffers remember him sitting in his tiny, spare office at the Bush headquarters on 15th Street, his cowboy boots propped up on his desk. He routinely carried a styrofoam cup to spit juice from the wad of chewing tobacco that bulged in his cheek. Strategy meetings were often punctuated with the sound of a stream hitting the bottom of his makeshift spittoon.

If George W. brought a bit of Midland style crossed with baseball culture to the nation's capital, he also brought the ethics of his newfound faith. During the 1988 campaign, an attractive young worker made it clear she was interested in Bush, and staffers began taking bets on whether the two would end up having an affair. Bush confronted the woman and backed her off in no uncertain terms. Later, a senior campaign official stormed into Bush's office to complain angrily that the woman had been humiliated.

"She's hurt," the official lashed out. "You really hurt her."

"Good, good," Bush replied evenly. "I'm a married man. I'm glad she got the signal."

To make sure that everyone understood his meaning, Bush usually traveled with an aide and asked the man to stay in his hotel room until late at night as a safeguard against rumors about women. He refused to be away from his wife and children more than two days at a time and often demanded to be flown home from campaigning only to spend the night and fly back the next day. "He wanted everyone to know that nothing was happening," the staffer said.[6]

It was not an act. Bush was on a flight one evening with a senator and a congressman. The two other men were downing Scotch and sodas and discussing how they kept their girlfriends from wives and journalists. The more they drank, the more eagerly they celebrated their trysts. Bush listened for a while, laughing where he could, and then said, "I'm a lucky man to have Laura." The senator and congressman went silent. Bush continued cheerily, "Let's toast Laura." So the three raised their glasses—the vice president's Bible-reading son and the two adulterous national leaders—to toast the Methodist librarian from Texas.[7]

Staffers soon learned to respect the candidate's son and to value what "Junior" brought to the campaign. He would be the "loyalty barometer," the man who made sure the troops stayed true. He was called "the Enforcer," and his famous tongue-lashings of staff and reporters became known as "feisting out." He was a moral force on the campaign, and this may be why it became his job to ride herd on the brilliant but volatile political strategist Lee Atwater. Their partnership would provide a needed education for both men.

—⁂—

When George W. first met Atwater at Camp David late in 1986, he cut through the customary pleasantries by asking, "How do we know we can trust you?" Jeb Bush put it even more directly: "What he means is, if someone throws a grenade at our dad, we expect you to jump on it." Their suspicions had been aroused by the fact that Atwater had business partners and friends who were working on other campaigns. "It made me very nervous," Bush recalls. Atwater was his typically flippant self and challenged Bush in return by saying, "If you're so worried about my loyalty, why don't you come to Washington and help me with the campaign? That way, if there's a problem, you'll be there to solve it."[8]

Bush agreed, but it did not take long for Atwater to misbehave. In the December issue of *Esquire* magazine, an article appeared entitled, "Why Is Lee Atwater So Hungry?" The piece captured Atwater in all his crass glory. He cursed. He talked about the joys of massage parlors. He did interviews while using the restroom. And he gave away secrets. When the story hit the newsstands, the campaign staff was livid. No one was angrier than Barbara Bush. She called her son and demanded he wring an apology from the errant strategist.[9] George W. fired away at Atwater, telling him, "You can't behave this way. You're representing a great man."[10] Within days, Barbara received a letter of apology. The taming of Lee Atwater had begun.

Yet, what Atwater lacked in social grace he made up for with political savvy. He understood that to wear the mantle of Ronald Reagan, the senior Bush was going to have to shed his hesitant style—what the press already called the "weenie" or "wimp" factor—and do battle like the old warrior Atwater knew he was. Bush could be a great man, he believed; he just had to be packaged right.

Atwater was the man to do it, the kind of campaign packager who made purists nervous. His mantra was "play dumb and keep moving." He knew how to build coalitions, how to frame issues according to interest group, and how to raise money. He also knew how to "stay out of the tall weeds"—keeping the candidate from controversy and complexity. Most of all, he knew how to play hardball, something the aristocratic senior Bush desperately needed to do. George W. watched, learned, countered when necessary, and remembered everything.

Aside from chaining himself to Atwater, George W. also served his father by handling the religious side of the campaign. Both because Pat Robertson was a candidate and because Ronald Reagan had mobilized them, conservative Christians were more a force to be reckoned with in the 1988 election than ever before. They were called the Religious Right, and they had been emerging for decades, a flowing together of usually parallel streams: evangelicals, the politically conservative members of mainline denominations, socially conscious Catholics, Charismatics, and Pentecostals stirred into action by Robertson, and all given new voice by the rise of religious broadcasters.

They came into the arena with a new language attached to a new agenda. They talked about being "born again" and about what they saw as the problem of secular humanism. They pointed out that the phrase "separation of church and state" appeared nowhere in the U.S. Constitution but did appear in the Soviet Constitution. They wanted to know why that assumed misapplication meant they could not pray in their schools, put the Ten Commandments in their statehouses, or endorse candidates in their sermons. They believed the Supreme Court sanctioned murder in its 1973 *Roe v. Wade* decision legalizing abortion and promoted atheism in denying pubic school students the right to read the Bible on their campuses. They wanted creationism taught alongside evolution in the public schools, textbooks that gave more than a nod to the nation's religious origins, and sex education left to parents.

Furthermore, they wanted their president to be a godly man. Jimmy Carter had talked about being born again but had disappointed most evangelicals. Though Carter at the least made faith in office fashionable, Ronald Reagan was their true hero. He talked about divine destiny, the rights of the unborn, and the influence of the Bible on his life. But despite his eight years in office, the Reagan administration had not made much progress on the issues religious conservatives cared about. They wanted a man who would use the presidency as a bully pulpit, face down the liberals, and make the country safe for faith once again.

They were not sure the senior Bush was their man. This new force in politics confused him. He believed, but he could not articulate his faith effectively. He sounded canned, stilted, and, worse, he came off like he was unsure. In George W., though, candidate Bush had a man who knew *his* mind but spoke *their* language. "His father wasn't comfortable dealing with religious types," recalled a staffer who worked on the evangelical issue. "George knew exactly what to do."[11] He knew because he was one of them. He had been schooled in the language and thinking of religious conservatives in the Community Bible Study program and through his relationships with fellow born-again politicos.

The man at George W.'s side to win the Religious Right was Doug Wead, a former Assemblies of God evangelist, friend of Jim and Tammy Faye Bakker, and a major player in the conservative Amway world. Wead's political influence had come largely through publishing. In 1980, he had written a short book on Ronald Reagan as a man of faith timed for release at the GOP National Convention. It had helped win the religious vote. He later worked with born-again entertainer Pat Boone and cowrote a book with Interior Secretary James Watt. He was also known in religious circles for having appeared on Bakker's television show dozens of times. Wead told the *Washington Post* that when he met the younger Bush, he knew immediately "that I wasn't going to have to write a 20-page memo explaining what 'born again' means."[12]

Wead helped George W. articulate the evangelical movement to the largely non-evangelical Bush campaign. In a manual entitled "The Vice President and the Evangelicals: A Strategy," Wead identified Robertson as the man to beat in the eyes of evangelicals and explained how the evangelical movement thinks and what it was looking for in a president. His work earned Wead the title "Liaison for Coalitions." George W. was so impressed, he told Wead, "You're mine. You report to me."[13]

With the strategy clear, the real work began. George W. flew around the country, often with Wead at his side, talking to religious leaders in a language they understood. He prayed with them, he articulated his father's faith, and he gave assurances. To press the message home, Wead wrote *Man of Integrity,* essentially a campaign biography wrapped in religious garb, designed to reach religious voters. Composed of a series of interviews, the book dealt heavily with the senior Bush's downing during World War II, his personal faith, his friendships among religious leaders, and his personal morals. It was everything the Religious Right wanted to hear, and when the book appeared at the Christian Booksellers' Association convention in 1988, it found a sympathetic audience.

The battle was far from won, though, and frustrations continued to mount. The faithful were not flocking to Bush, many preferring the more familiar Christianity of Pat Robertson. At one point, an irritated George W. announced at a rally, "There's more than one God-fearing man running for president of the United States." To make matters worse, there were rumors that the elder Bush had been involved in an affair. *Newsweek* and *U.S. News and World Report* picked up the story, and before long the Bush campaign was doing damage control. In the manner of the old school, some in the campaign counseled not to respond. Atwater knew better and told George W. he had to do something or he could write off the evangelicals.

The "dynamic duo," as some in the campaign now called them, flew into action. While Atwater scheduled an off-the-record lunch with Howard Fineman of *Newsweek*, George W. confronted his father to settle the matter once and for all. The elder Bush adamantly denied the charge. George W. believed him, and when he met with Fineman, he said, "The answer to the big question is NO."[14] It was the kind of quote that circulates rapidly in Washington, and the rumors soon died.

While George W. was winning the Religious Right for his father, Laura Bush knew that something else was happening as well. Working on the campaign meant a new kind of relationship for George W. and his father. It was "an opportunity to be an adult with an adult parent," Laura has said. "I think working with his dad, like George got to do in 1988...if there was any sort of leftover competition with being named George Bush and being the eldest son, that it really at that point was resolved."[15] If this was true, it was an important deliverance for him. He could not fulfill his growing sense of purpose haunted by the ghost of his father's achievements. Perhaps he meant more than others at the GOP National Convention knew when, as the head of the Texas delegation, he announced that the 111 Texas votes would go to the state's "favorite son and *the world's best father*."[16]

Equally tender, then, would be the family's private prayer time the day after his father's victory over Michael Dukakis. The Bush family met at St. Martin's Episcopal Church, their home church in Houston. George W. led the family in prayer and asked simply, "Many of us will begin a new challenge. Please give us strength to endure and the

knowledge necessary to place our fellow man over self...
please guide us and guard us on our journey, particularly
watch over Dad and Mother."[17]

As the Bush administration took over the White House,
many expected George W. to stay in Washington and enjoy
the spoils. He did help staff the new administration, and
from time to time his father did bring him in to handle particularly tough situations: The firing of John Sununu and
damage control around the ever-troubled Vice President Dan
Quayle are examples. But what most people did not know
was that a month before the election, George W. had heard
from one of his old Spectrum 7 investors that the Texas
Rangers baseball team was up for sale. Only those who
knew him best could possibly imagine what this might
mean to him.

—∙∙∙—

People who do not love baseball perhaps have difficulty
understanding the hold the country's "national pastime" has
on George W. Bush's heart. This is not surprising, for if the
game is not synonymous with all that is good in their lives
and if it has not become a tutor in life's dearest lessons, then
they cannot expect to revere it as he does. Maybe it is possible to understand his love for the game by simply tracing its
role in his life and by imagining how anything else so deeply
embedded in his history would also become a near religion to
him. It is an important exercise, for baseball is certainly as
important as Midland in knowing who George W. Bush is.

Consider: George W.'s grandmother, Dorothy, was a fiery,
competitive, godly woman who had a profound impact
upon him. She read aloud from the Bible every morning and
demanded so much of her children that she once chastised
her second son for his bad manners—even though he was

the president of the United States at the time. When the woman was pregnant with this same son, her contractions started during a family baseball game. But she would not stop playing. She took her turn at bat, hit a home run, and ran—yes, ran—the bases. Only after tagging home plate was she willing to leave for the hospital. The year was 1922. Pregnant women were not known for running out home runs.

Consider: Many of the men who modeled manhood for George W. in his early years were somehow connected to baseball. His grandfather, Prescott Bush, starred on the Yale team, as did his father: on the team that won the NCAA National Championship—twice. His great-uncle Buck was one of the owners of the New York Mets. As a boy, George W. met men most kids worshiped from afar—men like Casey Stengel and Rogers Hornsby.

Consider: When he was a boy in Midland, he hit upon a plan to have the best baseball card collection in town. These are, after all, the essential fuel for a boy's baseball dreams. He sent a letter to dozens of famous players asking them to sign their card, which he provided, and mail it back to him. He got autographed cards from Mickey Mantle, Willie Mays, and other greats of the game. The collection is worth thousands today. The bragging rights—and the dreams—are worth even more.

Consider: He watched as a teenager while the Houston Astrodome was built. It must have astounded him. Engineers said the design was not based on good science and the building would collapse. Feisty Judge Roy Hofheinz, the franchise owner, told the naysayers where they could go and built the thing any way. He not only gave the world a glorious cathedral of sport but also the largest indoor span it had known since the construction of Constantinople's famed Hagia Sophia in the sixth century—a new eighth wonder of the world. Imagine how such daring and inventiveness in the cause of sport must have thrilled a seventeen-year-old.

Consider: George W. played baseball almost every year of his youth. But he was never good enough. Never as good as his father. Never good enough to play varsity. Never a star. To love a game and be just fair at it when you have worshiped the game's heroes your whole life is to leave you—if you refuse to walk away in bitterness—with a reverence for the game that approaches worship.

Bush and baseball are intertwined. It is almost impossible to know his faith, his politics, or his loves without knowing his game. For example, in politics he is a traditionalist who believes the best of the past should be made to serve the future. In baseball, he believes—and tells students in a lecture on life's most important lessons—that "baseball should always be played outdoors, on grass, with wooden bats."[18] He's only half joking.

Baseball inspires Bush. When he talks about the game, he rises to his philosophical best. It is his natural religion, or maybe the earthly game that reveals his more mystical mind. Listen:

> Baseball inspires the Muses. Baseball does not have time limits or clocks; we are under no artificial deadlines except three outs to an inning. The true baseball fan loves the dull spots in a game, because they allow you to think and remember, to compare the present with the past. The competitor in me also loves the challenge of baseball, a challenge all of us identify with, because baseball is a sport played by normal-sized people. Joe Garagiola, former catcher and broadcaster, said, "Baseball gives you every chance to be great. Then it puts every pressure on you to prove that you

haven't got what it takes. It never takes away
that chance, and it never takes away that pressure."[19]

Columnist George Will has written that "Greek philoso-
phers considered sport a religious and civic—in a word,
moral—undertaking. Sport, they said, is morally serious
because mankind's noblest aim is the loving contemplation
of worthy things, such as beauty and courage. By witnessing
physical grace, the soul comes to understand and love beauty.
Seeing people compete courageously and fairly helps emanci-
pate the individual by educating his passions."[20] Perhaps those
who do not love baseball can simply accept that for those
who do the meaning is often about this inner work of the
game. It is indeed an emancipation, an ennobling contemplation of beauty. It is, in this sense, a religion, a passion for the
invisible. This too is part of the faith of George W. Bush.

—⁂—

It is easier, then, to imagine why when the opportunity
came to be part owner of the Rangers, Bush moved back to
Texas and worked tirelessly to make the deal happen. The
asking price was $80 million, and the seller was longtime
friend Eddie Chiles. Then in his mid-eighties, Chiles loved
his Rangers, despite their humiliating record, and wanted
the team to land in the right hands. He told Bush, "I'd like to
sell to you, son, but you don't have any money."[21]

It was true. To make the deal work, Bush would have to
draw investors. He assembled a group of the wealthy from
around the country and raised the needed money, but when
he approached Baseball Commissioner Peter Ueberroth, he
found that Ueberroth wanted half the investors to be
Texans. No problem. Bush scrambled again and got the right
men. Ueberroth consented. Buying the team would cost

Bush $600,000, nearly one-third of his entire net worth, and this was for "a team that had a twenty-five-year losing streak, sagging attendance and an inferior ballpark."[22] Bush loved the game so much, he thought it was a bargain.

The investors decided Bush should handle the team's day-to-day business, and he spent most of 1989 learning how things worked. The truth was that the Rangers were in trouble. The stadium had been designed for minor league play, and the team seemed mired in failure. Their record was abominable, and some wondered if the investors had known the state of things when they bought the franchise.

There were some bright spots, though. The Rangers were, in fact, one of the most storied franchises in modern major league baseball history—dating back to its early Washington Senators days. The team had boasted such legendary managers as Ted Williams, Whitey Herzog, Billy Martin, and Bobby Valentine. It had been the stage upon which Hall of Famer Nolan Ryan had achieved some of his most remarkable feats—including his three hundredth win, his record five thousandth strikeout, and two of his unparalleled seven no-hitters. Competing head-to-head with divisional rivals like the Oakland A's, the Seattle Mariners, and the Anaheim Angels, the American League team also has faced historic showdowns with perennial powers like the New York Yankees, the Boston Red Sox, the Detroit Tigers, and the Minnesota Twins.

Bush immediately put a uniquely Texas grassroots stamp on the institution. He had the team logo redesigned to reflect a more traditional design recalling the glory days of the old Texas Republic. He created the stunning Ballpark in Arlington for the club—one that not only reflects the ethos of the great ballparks of halcyon days gone by but also utilizes the distinctive elements of Texas vernacular architecture. In April

1994, when fans first walked under the rich green steel canopy, along the red brick arcade, and onto the wide open concourse overlooking the natural grass field, they could almost swear that both Abner Doubleday and Sam Houston would feel right at home.

David Schwarz, the architect Bush had chosen, had already gained a reputation for recovering that refined stockyard design legacy in several other major projects. He was thus a conspicuous choice—evidence that Bush was not only serious about turning the Rangers into a great franchise but also a genuine Texas cultural icon. Indeed, even the parking lots that surround the stadium were anointed with the Lone Star heritage—each lot is named for a different hero from the era of the Republic of Texas in the 1830s and 1840s.

When the park finally opened in 1994, no one loved it as he did. Rather than watch the games from an enclosed suite, which was standard practice for most owners, Bush preferred to sit with the fans. He said he wanted them to see him "sitting in the seat they sit in, eating the same popcorn, peeing in the same urinal."[23] He would position himself behind the Rangers dugout—Section 109, Row 1—and eat peanuts while he got to know the rowdiest fan, the hot dog vendors, and even the ticket-takers by their first names. Fans lined up for his autograph just as they did for Nolan Ryan.

There was a method to this ballpark reverie. Bush knew how to market. He got his parents to throw out the ball at a Rangers game when traditionally presidents did so only in Baltimore. He circulated pictures of his father wearing a Rangers cap. Fans would find it in their hearts to forgive him for letting Sammy Sosa get away on his watch only because every year he was in charge, attendance exceeded 2 million, and in time, the Rangers would win their division three times.

It is hard to exaggerate the meaning of all this to Bush. He told one reporter that people are always asking, "What's the boy ever done? Well, now I can say I've done something. Here it is."[24] It was not that he had accomplished something; it was that he had accomplished *this* thing. He had built a glorious temple to a human endeavor he loved. He had envisioned a thing and made it a reality. And it was a thing that made lives better, that added to a heritage of a sport he could not enhance by playing. He may have said it best when one day he walked up behind a friend at the ballpark and laid his chin on the other man's shoulder. Looking out over the "green surface shimmering under the fireball of a Texas sun, he purred, 'My own personal field of dreams.'"[25]

—⁂—

When George W. considered running for governor in 1990, he quickly came to the conclusion that he had not sufficiently distinguished himself to go after such a prize. He told a gathering of Dallas lawyers, "For now, I want to focus on my job as the managing general partner of the Texas Rangers and more importantly as a good father and good husband."[26]

By 1993, though, the picture had changed. The new stadium would open the next year, the Rangers were already on the rebound, Bush was becoming well known in Texas as the managing co-owner of the team, and, with his father's loss of the presidency to Bill Clinton in 1992, he no longer had a White House shadow over everything he did.

In the race for the governor's office, his opponent would be Ann Richards, the feisty Democrat who had won an upset victory over Republican Clayton Williams four years earlier. Richards had derided George W.'s father at the Democratic National Convention when she famously said in a nationally televised speech, "Poor George. He can't help it—he was born with a silver foot in his mouth."[27] The comment stung. Barbara Bush, watching on television, became physically ill when she heard it. George W. knew that if he ran against this sharp-witted lady, it would be a bitter fight.

He felt ready but had to convince his wife, and she had reservations. Laura knew that the loss of the presidency had hurt the Bush family, and she knew, too, that her husband lived in the shadow of his father's legacy. Neither were good reasons to run. George W. had to know that it was right for Texas and right for him, and until he did, she could not agree. She questioned, she probed, and sometimes she lectured. "She wanted to make sure this was something I really wanted to do," Bush said, "and that I wasn't being drug in as a result of friends or 'Well, you're supposed to do it in order to prove yourself, vis-à-vis your father.'"[28] When she had the assurance she needed, she "signed on."

Bush and his advisor, Karl Rove, designed a strategy early on that would set the tone for the campaign. They knew Richards was sharp-witted and that she was irritated by having to run against such an untested opponent. They expected the Bush candidacy would bring out the venom, and it did. She called Bush "Shrub," "the young Prince," "that young Bush boy," and joked that he was "missing his Herbert," a reference to his father's two middle names. In the heated last months of the campaign, Richards even exploded in anger: "You just work like a dog, you do well...and all of a sudden you've got some jerk who's running for public office telling everybody it's all a sham."[29]

Knowing Richards' volatility, Bush and Rove decided to take the opposite tack. As Bush told Rove, "We're never going to attack her because she would be a fabulous victim. We're going to treat her with respect and dignity. This is how we're going to win."[30] Or, as Bush later expressed it,

"We're going to kill her with kindness."[31] Thus, Bush never resorted to mud-slinging, never made personal attacks, and never responded in kind to her stinging barbs.

They also planned to win with a clear agenda. They knew that the elder Bush had lost the presidency in part because he did not have a clear focus. Meanwhile, Clinton's strategist kept their candidate on message with the phrase "It's the economy, stupid!" George W. learned the lesson. He campaigned on a four-point plan: return control of education to local school districts, toughen up juvenile-justice laws, design stricter provisions for welfare recipients, and reform the state's tort laws. He kept his message simple, and he repeated it as often as he could. As Richards told Larry King, "You know, if you said to George, 'What time is it?' he would say, 'We must teach our children to read.'"[32] If Bush was anything, he was "on message."

Religion also became a major theme in the campaign. Though both candidates were Methodists, they clearly came from different theological streams. In her 1989 autobiography, *Straight from the Heart*, Richards described the Lakeview Methodist Church she grew up in as "the center of all religious and social happenings."[33] Later in her life, though, Richards changed to the Unitarian Church, a denomination that denies much of the supernatural described in the Bible and views Jesus Christ only as an important historical figure.

When she entered treatment for alcoholism at St. Mary's Hospital in Minneapolis, Richards "learned a lot about spiritualism" and "found a better understanding of my need to commune with a higher power, with God. I relaxed with the idea that there is a spirit and a power that is greater than myself, and that if I will call on and work with that power there will be moments in my life when I will experience true serenity."[34]

The differences between Bush's evangelical Methodism and Richards' liberal Methodism played loudly in the press. Bush inadvertently kept the religious issue in play when an Austin reporter who was Jewish asked him if he believed that Jesus is the only way to heaven. He said, "Yes." As Bush recalls, "It was, of course, picked up and politicized—you know, 'Bush to Jews: Go to Hell.' It was very ugly. It hurt my feelings."[35]

It was an issue Bush had apparently been wrestling with for some time. He had even gotten into a friendly argument with his mother over it one day when she suddenly picked up the phone and posed the question to Billy Graham. "I happen to agree with what George says," Graham told her, "but I want to remind both of you to never play God. It is one thing to have your personal opinion and to believe it and to act accordingly. It's another thing to condemn your fellow man. That other thing is to play God."[36] After this conversation, Bush was more cautious.

The campaign was bruising, and as late as September polls showed Richards had 42.9 percent of the vote with Bush trailing at 41 percent. Few had expected Bush to do as well as he was then doing, but his "kill her with kindness" strategy was working. So was the character he was showing.

While on a dove hunt during the campaign, he accidentally shot a killdee, a protected songbird. Rather than cover up his error, he went before the press and said, "I have a confession to make; I'm a killdee killer." At a Dallas news conference later that day, he continued to poke fun at himself: "Thank goodness it was not deer season; I might have shot a cow."[37] Texans found such self-deprecating humor endearing. They also took note of his courage when he followed famed orator Barbara Jordan in an appearance at a black church in Houston. Jordan's magnificent voice filled the church as she said, "I am here because I support Ann Richards for governor of Texas." When it was his turn, Bush honored Jordan as the "epitome of a soldier for what is right." Then he grinned and said, "I just happen to disagree with her choice for governor."[38] Even the pastor smiled. Bush won the election, 53 to 46 percent.

—⁓—

Texans quickly learned that their new governor's leadership style was Reaganesque. He would set the vision, define the culture, fashion the team, set the boundaries, and stay out of the details. It was a style suited for his new role, for Texas required as little of its executive as any state in the union. Nevertheless, Bush would find himself dealing with some of the most politically and religiously charged issues in the state's history. The one that would haunt Bush's public life for years to come was the execution of convicted murderer Karla Faye Tucker.

On June 13 of 1983, Karla Tucker and her boyfriend, Daniel Garrett, entered Jerry Lynn Dean's apartment. Their plan was simply to take inventory for a future stealing spree. They had not expected to find Dean at home. High on drugs, Tucker and Garrett began beating Dean with a hammer and then a three-foot-long pickax. Dean's girlfriend, Deborah Thornton, hid under the bed sheets while Dean was murdered. She was soon discovered, and Tucker immediately hacked the woman to death with the pickax. She later bragged to friends that she experienced a sexual thrill while murdering Thornton. During the trial, she told the court that she had enjoyed it and felt no guilt.

Tucker was found guilty of murder and sentenced to death. Her boyfriend, Garrett, was also sentenced to death but died of liver disease in 1993. The case was bound to receive wide attention. If executed, Tucker would be the first woman put to death in Texas since 1863. But the case took an unexpected twist. In prison, Karla Tucker became a Christian and married the prison chaplain. She was a changed woman, she said, and her lawyers argued that she deserved clemency.

The case received nationwide attention. Moved by Tucker's conversion and her remarkably fruitful ministry among prisoners, religious leaders began calling for her release. Chief among them was Pat Robertson, whose Christian Coalition began mobilizing national support for Tucker. Governor Bush even received a letter from Pope John Paul II urging him against the death penalty. When Tucker appeared on *Larry King Live* and Americans saw a well-spoken, devout woman calmly pleading her case, Bush was besieged with letters and phone calls. His own daughters argued against Tucker's execution at the family dinner table.

Little by little, the conflict over Karla Faye Tucker grew ugly. Critics accused Bush of heartlessness and of failing his own Christian faith. *Talk* magazine reported that when Tucker appeared on *Larry King Live*, Bush had mocked the woman: "'Please,' Bush whimpers, his lips pursed in mock desperation, 'don't kill me.'"[39] Bush staffers adamantly denied this. Nevertheless, the anti-death-penalty lobby called Bush "the most-killing governor in the history of the United States of America."[40] The fact was that during Bush's time as governor, over 150 death-row inmates had been executed under Texas law, and it was not hard for some to blame this on the state's supposedly "bloodthirsty" governor. Political enemies began talking impeachment.

The crisis forced Bush to examine both the law and his beliefs. He knew that many of his critics were simply ill-informed about Texas law. Under the Texas Constitution, given the unanimous decision by the appeals board to proceed with the execution, the governor had no authority to commute a death sentence. He had two choices: allow the sentence, or grant a one-time thirty-day delay.

Bush also knew that he was being asked to act based on the religious conversion of an inmate. As sincere as Tucker might have been, jailhouse conversions were commonplace, and if he were to act in Tucker's case based on her conversion to Christianity, how could he refuse to do so if an inmate converted to another religion and made the same claim? It was beyond the range of human wisdom and beyond the scope of the law, Bush came to believe.

In a final public statement, he said, "Like many touched by this case, I have sought guidance through prayer. I have concluded judgments about the heart and soul of an individual on death row are best left to a higher authority. Karla Faye Tucker has acknowledged she is guilty of a horrible crime. She was convicted and sentenced by a jury of her peers. The role of the state is to enforce our laws and to make sure all individuals are treated fairly under those laws…therefore I will not grant a thirty-day stay. May God bless Karla Faye Tucker, and may God bless her victims and their families." Bush remembers the time it took to execute Karla Faye Tucker as "the longest twenty minutes of my tenure as governor."[41]

The Tucker crisis might very easily have been a last straw for Bush. He had been wronged in the name of religion by Kent Hance in his first congressional race. He had seen religion used in attempts to harm his father in the 1988 presidential race. Now he found himself vilified and called unchristian because he would not presume to know the heart of a convicted criminal or to acknowledge that it made any difference under the law. It would have been easy for

Bush to become a strict separationist at this point and allow no room for religion in public policy. Surprisingly, he did not do that, and in fact, chose to move the other way.

—∞—

For decades conservatives had been talking about the need to welcome volunteers, particularly religious volunteers, in the battle against the nation's social ills. It made no sense, they insisted, to disallow religious organizations to receive federal funding when they were often more effective in dealing with some problems than the state was. Moreover, interpreting the First Amendment as a ban on religious influence in social services was silly, they protested. They became adept at citing little known facts of American history: Some of the Founding Fathers had funded missionary outreaches to the Indians and for the printing of the Bible. Federal buildings in Washington, D.C., were once used as churches. The Northwest Ordinance made special provisions for educational institutions designed specifically to spread the Christian religion. Surely things had gone too far and to the detriment of the poor, the illiterate, and the drug addicted. It was time for a change, they insisted.

It was this very unshackling of volunteerism that President George H. W. Bush had meant by his "thousand points of light," a theme echoed by Newt Gingrich and Bill Bennett. George W. had also sounded the trumpet in Texas when he called for a society committed to individual responsibility and reliance on God rather than slavish reliance on government. It was Marvin Olasky, though, in his *The Tragedy of American Compassion,* who gave conservatives a blueprint for genuine reform.

Olasky had once been a Marxist but later underwent a conversion to Christianity. Rethinking his social views in the years before he was a professor at the University of Texas, Olasky came to the conclusion some others had reached: The war on poverty had only made poverty worse, government is not the only answer, social needs were once met by religious organizations, and it is time for that force for good to be unleashed again. As editor of *World* magazine and a noted syndicated columnist, Olasky's voice was increasingly being heard even before *The Tragedy of American Compassion* appeared in 1992.

Bush first became aware of Olasky when he read an article he had written in the *Wall Street Journal* about a crisis in his own state. In 1995, the state of Texas had begun to threaten an organization called Teen Challenge with fines and closure if it did not conform to licensing requirements for its drug and alcohol counselors. Teen Challenge operated drug treatment centers with counselors who were held to strict internal standards but who were not licensed professionals. Even though the organization could show long-term cure rates of 67 to 85 percent, far beyond that of any state program, Teen Challenge was in danger. "Outcomes and outputs are not an issue for us," a Texas Commission on Alcohol and Drug Abuse official famously said.[42]

Olasky's article, which appeared in the August 15 edition of the *Wall Street Journal*, described a protest in front of the historic Alamo led by graduates of the Teen Challenge programs. Signs held by participants read "Because of Jesus I Am No Longer a Debt to the State of Texas" and "Once a Burden, Now a Taxpayer." When Bush read the article, he realized that the protesters were calling for the very faith and personal responsibility for which he had campaigned—and that he had personally experienced. Unfortunately, it now appeared that his own state officials were standing in the way.

A short time later, Bush met with Olasky and began to

investigate how to make the needed changes. In time, he would persuade the Texas legislature to pass a bill that permitted faith-based institutions to opt out of certain state licensing requirements. And that was not all he did. Olasky later described the flurry of reforms Bush initiated:

> He issued an Executive Order making Texas the first state to establish the option of using private and religious charities to deliver welfare services. He set up a level playing field for both religious and nonreligious groups for Texas social service contracts, abstinence education grants, and poverty-fighting initiatives. He made Texas the first state to permit a state prison unit to be operated by a ministry. He established alternative licensing procedures for many faith-based programs. He created a pilot program establishing Second Chance group homes for unwed teen welfare mothers run by faith-based and other private groups. He proposed and signed a Good Samaritan law that gives liability protection to health professionals who donate charitable care to needy Texans. He recommended and signed a law requiring governmental agencies to develop welfare-to-work partnerships with faith-based groups in a way that respects those groups' unique religious character.[43]

Even detractors soon realized that Bush was actually doing what conservatives had talked about in theory for decades. His most memorable sentence from the time— "Government can do certain things very well, but it cannot put hope in our hearts or a sense of purpose in our lives"— captured not only his own thinking but the very heart of the conservative movement.[44] When Ronald Reagan spoke of getting government off the backs of the people, this was part of what he meant. When Reagan's vice president spoke of a new day of volunteerism, reforms like these were what he was hoping for. Even Bush's critics admitted that some cooperation was needed between private and state services. The Texas model was not the only option, but it was a step—a bold and creative step—led by a governor who had every reason to doubt that religion and government could ever work together effectively.

—⚭—

We should note the year. It is 1995. Slightly more than eleven years before, George W. was an oilman in crisis asking Arthur Blessitt how to follow Jesus. Since then, he has exited the world of oil, helped his father become president of the United States, purchased a baseball franchise, built a monument to baseball tradition and marketing, and become the reform-minded conservative governor of a state with an economy so large that if it were a nation, it would be the eleventh largest in the world.

In a few years he will write a book containing the words "My faith frees me," introduced by the sentence "I could not be governor if I did not believe in a divine plan that supersedes all human plans."[45] Whatever else he might mean by that statement, he will surely be thinking of his own life. He cannot have forgotten what he made of his life in the first forty years. Yet once he found faith, he became a man set free—from his lesser self, from the expectations of others, from a haunting hollowness. In just a decade, he has gone from a failed oilman to a man making history. Already he senses a "drawing," what he will term a "call," to a role he could not have seriously imagined just a decade before. And now, but just now, his faith frees him to say *yes* to that call.

Humble reliance: The presidential candidate prays with
James and Betty Robison on the set of the daily television
program *Life Today* in February 1999.

CHAPTER SIX

To Build a House of Faith

The candidate says he is "born again." He says he was raised to believe by Christian parents, and then he made a decision of his own later in life. He was baptized with his wife after they married, and the two have regularly attended church with their children ever since. "I freely acknowledge the role of faith in my life," he affirms, "and the centrality of faith in my belief system."[1]

Faith is essential to authentic living, he maintains, and it's time for nonbelievers to stop "making people who do believe in God feel like they're being put down." He believes also that his country has a divine destiny to fulfill: "[America] is serving as I believe God meant us to—as a light to this ever-shrinking world."[2] What is more, the candidate thinks religion has a rightful place in politics. "I believe strongly in the separation of church and state," he says, "but freedom *of* religion need not mean freedom *from* religion."[3]

That's why the candidate is proposing to fund faith-based organizations with federal dollars. "For too long," he explains, "faith-based organizations have wrought miracles on a shoestring. With the steps I'm proposing today they will no longer need to depend on faith alone."[4]

Not only is the candidate proposing federal support for faith-based institutions, but he wants corporations to pitch in as well. "I call on the corporations of America to encourage and match contributions to faith-and-values-based organizations."[5] Indeed, his stand amounts to a pillar of his campaign. "Today I give you this pledge," he affirms. "If you elect me your president, the voices of faith-based organizations will be integral to the policies set forth in my administration."[6]

The candidate is resolute. He feels his stand is historic. His faith compels him to act.

And his name is Al Gore.

—m—

Religion was seldom far from center stage in the 2000 presidential race. Bush was bold to say that Jesus had saved him. Gore wanted people to know he had always been a Baptist. Bush needed people to know he wasn't the playboy he once had been. Gore wanted to distance himself from the morally questionable Clinton years. Bush intended to extend the same welcome to faith-based organizations at the federal level that he had in Texas. Gore said he thought it was a good plan, and that, in fact, it was his idea first. The issue of faith was so prevalent that one writer quipped, "God may retire from politics after this election."

That Bush was so vocal about his sense of calling and his personal faith during the campaign belies the fact that his decision to run had not come easily. There had long been talk of him vindicating his father's loss of the presidency to Clinton. *Vanity Fair* even quoted Bush as telling a friend who doubted that he could beat Ann Richards, "I'm not runnin' against her, I'm runnin' against the guy in the White House."[7] Yet the various accounts of Bush's decision to run reflect a slower, more spiritual process.

His friend Paul O'Neill is certain that the idea of running for president never entered Bush's mind until George Shultz anointed him. Shultz had been secretary of state under Ronald Reagan, and when he met Bush in California shortly after his second win in Texas, Shultz turned to Bush and said, "I think you ought to be president. Twenty-five years ago Reagan stood in the same spot, and I said the same thing to him."[8] Shultz began telling other conservatives that "this young man" would be the next Ronald Reagan.[9]

Bush remembers that around that same time he was sitting in Highland Park Methodist Church in Dallas. The pastor, Mark Craig, was preaching on Moses' reluctance to lead God's people. Craig had just visited Old Faithful in Yellowstone Park and noticed that people applauded every time the geyser erupted with the regularity it had maintained for centuries. They were applauding faithfulness, the pastor said in his sermon. Moses tried to avoid being faithful. When God called Moses to deliver his people, he responded, "Sorry, God, I'm busy. I've got a family. I've got sheep to tend. I've got a life."[10] Eventually, though, Moses relented and delivered a nation.

Bush recalls that once the pastor set this scene in the Bible, he pressed his point hard. People are "starved for leadership," Craig said, "starved for leaders who have ethical and moral courage." The pastor continued, and as he did, Bush began to sense that there was a message meant for him beyond the words of a man. He felt a "call," a sense that God was directing him to run for president. As if she knew what he was sensing, Bush's mother, Barbara, turned to him after the sermon and said, "He was talking to you."[11] Not long after, Bush called James Robison and told him, "I've heard the call. I believe God wants me to run for president."[12]

The relationship between Bush and Robison had begun sometime before when talk first began to circulate that Bush might be the man for the White House. The two men had happened upon each other from time to time during the Reagan and Bush presidencies. Robison had not been impressed at first. He thought of George W. as a "party boy," a man "making a buck," and a "sports nut." He could not have been more shocked when Bush ran for governor, then won, and then did a "commendable job."[13] He was astonished, too, when he realized that Bush was becoming a serious possibility for a presidential run. He knew he had to meet this man, so he made arrangements to see Bush while traveling through Austin with his wife, Betty.

It would not be Robison's first venture into the corridors of political power. Born the product of a rape and raised by his mother in poverty, Robison had the type of hardscrabble, "disadvantaged-boy-makes-good" testimony that is the stuff of legends. By the 1970s, he was becoming one of America's best-known evangelists. Some spoke of him as the heir to Billy Graham's mantle.

Besides his preaching ministry, Robison had a gift for networking, for gathering people to pray and discuss the nation's problems who might otherwise never have associated with one another. He was particularly adept at connecting the Religious Right with conservative politicians and was even instrumental in encouraging Ronald Reagan to run for president in 1980. He had also challenged and prayed with the senior Bush during his years in office, a memory that must have occurred to the governor of Texas when he found out that Robison wanted to see him.

On the day that the evangelist entered Bush's office, he was surprised to find political strategist Karl Rove there as well, and even more surprised at what Bush was about to say. "My life is changed," the governor said. "I had a drinking problem. I won't say I was an alcoholic, but it affected my relationships, even with my kids. It could have destroyed me. But I've given my life to Christ."[14]

Robison, who had heard rumors of Bush's conversion, was struck by the sincerity he sensed. He was not prepared, though, for what came next. "I feel like God wants me to run for president," Bush said. "I can't explain it, but I sense my country is going to need me. Something is going to happen, and, at that time, my country is going to need me. I know it won't be easy, on me or my family, but God wants me to do it."[15]

"In fact," Bush continued, "I really don't want to run. My father was president. My whole family has been affected by it. I know the price. I know what it will mean. I would be perfectly happy to have people point at me someday when I'm buying my fishing lures at Wal-Mart and say, 'That was our governor.' That's all I want. And if I run for president, that kind of life will be over. My life will never be the same. But I feel God wants me to do this, and I must do it."[16]

There was other conversation, about Bush's past and what the campaign might hold for him. Before he left, Robison asked Bush if he would be willing to meet with religious leaders from "across racial and denominational lines."[17]

"I'm talking about strong men," Robison said, "men who will speak straight to you. Would you let them pray with you, and would you hear their hearts?"[18]

"I'd like it very much," Bush said, and then he turned to Rove and said, "Karl, let's do this."[19]

Robison shook hands and left. As he left the capitol, he was trembling. He got in his car, took his wife's hand, and said, "I had no idea I was going to hear what I have heard. I feel like the destiny of the world has been touched today. I feel just like I did in that hotel room in Atlanta."[20]

Betty Robison knew that her husband was recalling a conversation he had with Ronald Reagan years before. After a time of prayer, Robison turned to Reagan and said, "Governor, is Jesus real to you?" With the bobbing of the head and the opening word that became so familiar, Reagan said, "Well...my father was an alcoholic. My mother was the greatest influence in my life. And Jesus is more real to me than my mother." Robison believed when he left Reagan's presence that he had just spoken to the future president of the United States, a man who would preserve freedom. It was the same now after his conversation with Bush.[21]

True to his word, Robison began to introduce Bush to religious leaders. One meeting, on April 15, 1999, was typical. Bush arrived at Oak Cliff Bible Fellowship, pastored by nationally known black preacher Tony Evans, to meet with pastors from a wide variety of backgrounds: Pentecostal, Southern Baptist, and Charismatic, among others. The meeting lasted about ninety minutes, and by the time Bush was done talking and fielding questions, the pastors there began to feel that he was not just another politician peddling religion for votes. Before the meeting ended, the pastors gathered around Bush and laid hands on him. While the governor's security people watched nervously, the pastors prayed that God would bless him and his family, keeping him humble and always in God's hand. Some noticed that there were tears in Bush's eyes during the prayer.

At a similar gathering in Austin, this one involving both business leaders and clergymen, Bush found himself seated next to Bishop Keith Butler, pastor of the 18,000-member Word of Faith International Christian Center in Southfield, Michigan. During lunch, Bishop Butler turned to the candidate and asked, "Gov. Bush, are you born again?"

Without hesitation, Bush replied, "Yes."

"How do you know it?" Butler pressed.

Bush said he had acted upon the biblical truth of Romans 10:9, then quoted the verse word for word: "That if thou shalt confess with thy mouth the Lord Jesus, and shalt believe in thine heart that God hath raised him from the dead, thou shalt be saved."

"I've been changed inside," he acknowledged to Butler. "My life has been transformed. Jesus is my Lord." The words impressed Bishop Butler, who was moved by this clear affirmation of faith to support Bush for president.[22]

There were other such gatherings. One of the most memorable took place in Ed Young Jr.'s Fellowship Church in the Dallas area. Again, a diverse group had assembled, ranging from Word of Faith preacher Kenneth Copeland to more mainline Baptists and Methodists. When the governor finished speaking, the group asked if they could lay hands on him, and San Antonio pastor David Walker prayed simply for God to "put the mantle of a champion" on Bush. "Nobody said he would be the next president," Walker said afterward, "but it was obvious that this man's heart gravitates toward the things of the Lord."[23]

Many at the meeting felt the way that Robison did about Bush. As he later said, "Governor Bush doesn't want to use God to get elected. He doesn't want to ride in on a God plank. He just wants God to use him."[24]

Not everyone was convinced. From the time Bush first

came under consideration for a presidential run, analysts doubted that he and the Religious Right would be a good fit. "I don't think that George W. Bush would be the favored candidate of the Religious Right under any circumstances," said John C. Green, professor at the University of Akron and an expert on the Religious Right in American politics. "He's too moderate for them. He could be their second choice, or their third or fourth or fifth. That's the big question."[25]

Bush's perceived middle-of-the-road politics were more than a question for some members of the Religious Right. James Dobson, of Focus on the Family, publicly chastised Bush for not supporting a pro-life amendment to the Constitution. Bush had long believed that abortion laws were not going to change until there was first a change in culture. This sounded like fence-sitting to Dobson, and he said so. Robison called Dobson and pleaded with him not to be a "political kingmaker" but to try to understand "what God might be doing" through Bush.[26] Dobson agreed and, in time, chose to support Bush. Not long after, Pat Robertson weighed in, saying that Bush was the most electable candidate carrying the flag for the issues conservative Christians cared about. After these endorsements, Bush enjoyed strong support from the religious wing of the Republican Party.

—⁜—

And so began the candidacy of George W. Bush for the presidency of the United States. There would be the crowds and the signs and the handshakes and the speeches. There would be the buses and the planes and jogging before the cameras. He would answer questions, he would debate, and he would famously mangle the English language. He would speak at Bob Jones University, a Christian school that did not allow interracial dating, and his opponents would try to make him out to be a Bible-thumping racist. Senator John McCain would blast Bush for his visit to Bob Jones and then go on to indict leaders of the Religious Right as "agents of intolerance" and "forces of evil."[27] Bush would answer questions about his distant past until he could hardly do it graciously.

He would make mistakes. He would use coarse language to describe a journalist only to find that his microphone was on and the whole nation heard. He had been abroad only three times in his life, and he had not paid much attention to foreign policy, so he could not name key world leaders when a reporter asked him to. People began to question his intelligence. That made him angry. He became sharp at times. He told people he did not care whether he became president or not, and then asked for their vote. Naturally, they were confused. And just before Election Day, the nation found out he had been charged with drunk driving as a young man and he had not disclosed it during the campaign. The press saw shades of Clinton.

But there were high points, too. He held his own in the big, televised debates—if only because Al Gore came across like the class know-it-all. He chose Dick Cheney as his running mate, which gave the ticket the foreign policy *gravitas* it needed. He got better at giving speeches and gave the best one of his life at the GOP National Convention, where it counted most. He learned to speak from the gut. Even hard-edged commentators like Joe Klein said, "He used words like *love* and *heart* more than any other presidential candidate I've ever seen."[28] He was doing what he had always done: morphing, adapting, improving on himself, letting failure motivate and teach.

And then, when it all should have been over, it wasn't. Gore conceded and then didn't. Bush won and then found he hadn't. It was nerve-wracking. There were hanging chads and the official declaration of victory by Florida Secretary of State Katherine Harris, and the country learning that it had an Electoral College. Then there were the courts and that amazing evening when Al Gore showed such grace and spoke with such poetry—something rarely seen in American politics. And George W. Bush became the forty-third president of the United States of America.

—◊◊◊—

But why did Bush win? He was not the candidate with the widest appeal, nor did he have the broadest experience. In fact, he won with one of the thinnest résumés of any president in American history. He very possibly was not, as one columnist sniffed, the "sharpest knife in the drawer." And he made his mistakes. So how did he defeat the two-term vice president of a relatively popular president?

Exit polls showed that Bush beat Gore by fifteen points among married people with children and by seventeen points among people who attend church weekly. Gore finished nineteen points higher among women who work outside the home and twenty-nine points higher among people who never attend church at all. Clearly, faith and family were factors.[29]

Yet, according to the polls, character was a primary issue, too. When asked "What is the most important thing to consider when you decide who to vote for?", one-quarter of all voters answered, "Honesty." Of this one-quarter, 80 percent voted for Bush.[30]

Presidential speechwriter David Frum has explained, "Bush's base liked his tax-cut plan. They supported him on missile defense, on Social Security reform, on faith-based charities, even (if less enthusiastically) on education. But what they most wanted from him was something much simpler: They wanted him not to be Clinton."[31]

Bush stepped onto the presidential stage when America still remembered the nobility of the Reagan/Bush era but had since lived through eight years of Clinton. They thought of Clinton in the terms historian Stephen Ambrose once used to describe Thomas Jefferson, as a "great mind with a limited character."[32] They wanted a change. They had endured rule by "the best and the brightest." Now they wanted rule by the good, and they believed that Bush was the man who could make it happen. In a choice between immoral brilliance and the C student with a moral compass, they would take the moral compass.

—⁂—

As if to say he got the voters' message, Bush's inaugural address sounded the call to a new purity. "Our public interest depends on private character," he proclaimed. "I will live and lead by these principles: 'to advance my convictions with civility, to pursue the public interest with courage, to speak for greater justice and compassion, to call for responsibility and try to live it as well.' In all of these ways, I will bring the values of our history to the care of our times."[33]

The covenant made, Bush promptly set to work. Columnist Peggy Noonan reflected the thinking of many supporters of the new administration when she suggested that Bush make his first act in the White House an exorcism: "I think that all places of concentrated power have within them the devil's little imps—little imps, unseen, sitting on the cornice of the doorway in this office, giggling quietly in a corner on a bookcase in that one....All White Houses have them. But in the one just ending the imps ran wild. It would be a very good and important thing if Mr. Bush invited in a fine and good priest, a wise and deep rabbi, a faithful and loving minister, and had them pray together in that house, and reanoint it, and send the imps, at least for a while, on their way."[34]

Whether Bush thought of his moving into the White House in terms of a reanointing or not, he clearly set out to break from the spirit of the previous administration. On his first day in the Oval Office, Bush suspended dozens of eleventh-hour executive orders made by Bill Clinton. He also reinstated the Mexico City Policy, which cut off taxpayer support for international abortion services. The policy had been instituted by Reagan but overturned by Clinton. In a sense, Bush was bringing Reagan back. It would not be the last time.

Bush then declared the next Sunday a National Day of Prayer and Thanksgiving and halted all hiring until his cabinet members were in place. It would not take long. The Senate confirmed seven of his nominees three hours after he submitted them.

Before the sun set on his first day, the president signed an order establishing ethical standards for his new administration. The order called for anyone working in his government to "maintain the highest standards of integrity" and spelled out specific rules prohibiting the use of public office for private gain, holding financial interest that conflicted with official duties, and forbidding discriminatory practices.[35] Some believed his first day was the dawning of a new day for the country.

—m—

Key to the continuance of this new day was Bush's leadership team. Critics had said the born-again president would feel compelled to choose a cabinet of preachers. It would be the Elmer Gantry administration. They were soon surprised. The Bush administration would be the most diverse in history, positioning, for example, more African Americans and Hispanics in prominent positions than any previous administration.[36]

The same was true for women. In an article on presidential advisor Karen Hughes, *Esquire* reported, "The Left is loath to acknowledge that its long-held dream for a woman to have such power—in this case leading a sorority of more senior staff and cabinet-level women than in any administration in U.S. history—has somehow occurred on a Republican watch."[37] It was true, but the changes did not stop there. Some observed that a Bush cabinet meeting was so racially diverse that it looked like a committee meeting at the United Nations.

Still, the critics were right about one thing: The Bush people were more often than not people of faith. There was Presbyterian minister's daughter and brilliant foreign policy expert, Condoleezza Rice. John Ashcroft, a former senator and now attorney general, was a faithful member of the Assemblies of God. Chief of Staff Andrew Card was married to a Methodist minister. Commerce Secretary Don Evans had been with Bush since the days of the Community Bible Study in Midland. And Karen Hughes, the one they called "The Prophet," was a Presbyterian elder. And there were dozens like them at every level of the administration.

What distinguished the Bush brand of the faithful was that they did not leave their spiritual lives at the door of the White House. David Frum, who is Jewish, said that the first words he ever heard spoken in the Bush White House were, "Missed you at the Bible study."[38] Since 1997, federal regulations had allowed religious activities in government workplaces so long as the nonreligious were not harassed or pressured.[39] Bible studies and prayer meetings in federal buildings became commonplace and nowhere more than in the White House. As one staffer said, "No one assumes the White House is a church, and no one thinks they can slack off on their work in the name of religion. But we do understand that the political vision we serve is fueled by faith, and the nation benefits when there are brown-bag Bible studies and before-work prayer meetings in the White House."[40]

Yet nothing signaled a new day in Washington quite like George W. Bush himself. He seemed determined to be the exemplar of his own moral vision. He opened every cabinet meeting with prayer and insisted on a high moral tone. A story from David Frum illustrates: "Early in my White House stint, somebody asked me at a meeting whether I was sure of something. I said I was. He pressed me: 'Are you *sure?*' Irritated, I replied emphatically: 'Yes, I am damn sure.' The temperature in the room suddenly seemed to drop about a dozen degrees. There was a prolonged silence as I tried to figure out my mistake. I got it. 'Er—I mean, yes indeed, I am quite sure.'"[41] The Bush White House would be a largely teetotaling, nonsmoking, noncussing affair. The drug of choice would be M&M's.

Bush seemed intent on being the honest man the voters hoped for. If he was recording a radio speech in Washington to be aired while he was in Oklahoma, he refused to say, "Today, I'm in Oklahoma." He would stop recording, pull down his glasses, and protest, "But I'm not in Oklahoma." Speechwriters learned not to insert "I'm happy to be here" in a speech. If the president was not happy, he would not read the line. And once when he was scheduled to fly to Florida and take credit for a huge project to restore the Everglades, he simply said, "Today I signed an Everglades agreement with the state of Florida. It's legislation that passed prior to my time." That a president would not take credit for a multibillion-dollar project, no matter whose idea it was, left Washington-watchers incredulous.[42]

Yet even those who missed the subtle signals of his character could not miss the times he welcomed, even encouraged, spiritual devotion. The most notable of these was on Palm Sunday of 2002. The president and his team were flying back from El Salvador aboard Air Force One. Knowing that he hated to miss church, members of his cabinet suggested to the president that they organize a worship service in the air. Bush agreed.

Before long, there were nearly forty officials crammed into the plane's conference room. Condoleezza Rice, an accomplished classical musician, led the worship. Karen Hughes gave the lesson, and the entire affair ended with the singing of "Amazing Grace" and hugs and kisses as a sign of Christian fellowship.

Later, Bush remembered, "You know, I did feel the presence of God amongst my friends on Air Force One. There were a lot of people on the plane, and to be able to worship with people with whom you work in a unique spot is a special moment."[43]

Peggy Noonan would have been pleased. The imps were clearly on the run.

—⚉—

During his days in Community Bible Study in Midland, Bush had begun the discipline of daily devotions, a practice he carried with him into the White House. Every morning before dawn, even before he brought Laura a cup of coffee, he read from the Bible. Using the skills he learned in CBS, he examined each word of the passages he read, considered their context, meditated on their meaning for his life, and turned the words to prayer.

He found the Book of Psalms particularly invigorating. That poetic section in the heart of the Old Testament articulated the battles and the rewards of faith, the triumphs and the struggles of hope, the joys and the sorrows of love. His favorites were Psalms 27 and 91—passages that resonated with themes of moral steadfastness in the face of conflict.

He also read each day a selection from *My Utmost for His Highest,* the classic devotional work by Oswald Chambers. It has deeply impacted his thinking, the themes of each daily reading often showing up both in his public statements and his private conversation. It is not surprising that Bush loves the book as he does. Chambers wrote the classic while ministering to soldiers, and the illustrations he used are drawn from sports, the military, and nature, very much the language Bush speaks.

My Utmost for His Highest is a phenomenon of Christian literature. Published in 1923 after Chambers' death, it has remained continually in print ever since. With millions of copies in more than two dozen languages, it has become one of the best-selling inspirational books of all time—a classic on a par with John Bunyan's *Pilgrim's Progress.*

Chambers was born in Scotland in 1874—in the same year G. K. Chesterton and Winston Churchill were born. His father was a Baptist pastor, converted and trained under the ministry of Charles Haddon Spurgeon, arguably the most influential English Christian of the nineteenth century. His mother was converted under the ministry of Thomas Chalmers, who was likewise the most influential Scottish Christian of the age. This rich spiritual legacy was evident in the writing and teaching of Chambers. The resulting humble simplicity, deep piety, and passionate vision ultimately encouraged Christians to live their lives as "broken bread and poured out wine" for Christ, to "give their utmost for His highest."[44]

Bush's disciplined reading and meditation in the little devotional cannot help but affect how he views his presidency. Chambers insisted that men ought to view their gifts in life as sacred trusts to be exercised for the good of others. Everything a man possesses, from his money to the authority he wields, is a tool for good in God's hands. It is an old Puritan perspective and one that Bush is drinking in daily as he seeks to fulfill the duties of the modern presidency.

—⚬—

In the spring of his first year in office, Bush gave a speech that foreshadowed much that was to come in his administration.[45] The occasion was a dinner at the American Jewish Committee convention in Washington. It would be a high-profile event, with Mexican president Vicente Fox, Israeli foreign minister Shimon Peres, and German foreign minister Joschka Fischer in attendance. Considering the AJC's history of defending religious minorities worldwide, and given their uniquely Jewish concerns as well, the invitation offered Bush an opportunity to clarify some of his more controversial positions.

Bush knew that the Jewish community in America had serious reservations about his faith-based initiatives. They were suspicious of his born-again brand of Christianity and nervous that his "cowboy" style would allow him to run rough-shod over the church/state distinctions that most Jews in America held dear.

The whole plan was easily misunderstood. Bush wanted to fund religious institutions to tend the kind of social ills that are connected to the troubled human soul—problems like alcoholism and drug abuse. Yet, he did not want to fund those organizations to spread their beliefs. It was a subtle distinction but one that he had to make for faith-based initiatives to survive.

It was also a distinction Bush knew the Founding Fathers had made. He had heard much on this subject from conservative political thinkers like Marvin Olasky and his own speechwriter, David Gerson, among others. The First Amendment was designed to prevent the establishment of a state church. The colonists had known state-sponsored Anglicanism under English rule and found it wanting. But there was nothing in the First Amendment or anywhere else in the Constitution to prohibit federal encouragement of religion in general. This is where the practices of the Founders seemed more consistent with Bush's plans than with recent Supreme Court rulings.

Though the framers of the Constitution would have nothing to do with a state church in specific, they thought nothing of funding religion in general. With federal funds, the very men who ratified the Constitution appointed chaplains, printed Bibles, and even funded missionary endeavors to the Indians. One such act, in 1796, ordained special lands for the use of Christian Indians in a directive entitled "An Act regulating the grants of Land for propagating the Gospel among the Heathen."[46] On weekends, federal buildings in Washington were used as churches by a variety of denominations without any sense of injustice to the law. In fact, the Old Supreme Court chambers were used on Sunday mornings by Washington's First Presbyterian Church. Clearly, the Founding Fathers welcomed a connection between faith and government but jealously guarded the line between the institutional church and the state.

Bush saw his plan for faith-based initiatives as a return to the original design. Yet he could understand how a religious minority might view these initiatives as an open door to state-sponsored religious preference. To allay fears, once the opening pleasantries of his speech were concluded, he got right to the point.

"I took a look at this weekend's program before coming here," he said. "I was flattered to read that 'understanding the new administration' is called a 'central feature' of this year's meeting. Well, I may be able to save you some time." There was laughter. Everyone knew the president was cutting to the chase.

Then it came. "I believe that our government should support works of charity that are motivated by faith." There was a brief pause, and some may have felt a twinge of discomfort at the president's blunt opening line. He did not hesitate long, though, before reassuring, "But our government should never fund the teaching of faith itself."

It was a good beginning, but he was just getting started. The next issue was Israel, and everyone knew it had to come. Bush had spoken often of his "support" for Israel, but American Jews saw little of substance in his actions. They were confused. Bush was the political champion of evangelical America, the strongest concentration of support for Israel outside of the Jewish community itself.

Yet, he seemed to be abandoning the peace process and acting as though, as David Frum put it, "peace was something to be prayed for—rather than won on the battlefield or negotiated at a peace conference—[and] that could easily be interpreted as indifference to Israel's fate, or worse than indifference."[47] Already, Bush was on the way to canceling more international treaties in the first year of his presidency than any other executive in American history. Some in the audience wondered whether his commitments to Israel might suffer, too.

Bush was feeling the pressure, too. Even his administration was divided, with the Defense Department urging him to support Israel while his State Department championed the cause of the Arab nations. Conservatives were also split. Concerned about the influence of Israel in the nation's capital, Pat Buchanan had referred to Capitol Hill as an "Israeli occupied zone."[48] Meanwhile, other prominent conservatives unceasingly called for America to support Israel at all costs.

Bush knew, too, that his religious base was divided. Some Christians believe that the modern state of Israel no longer has the same place in God's economy as it did in the Old Testament. In this view, Israel should be esteemed as a favored U.S. friend and the lone democracy in the Middle East, but little more.

Other Christians, though, believe the modern nation of Israel is as much God's uniquely chosen people as they were in ancient times. In this view, modern Israel is the rightful heir of a vast region divinely granted to them since the time of the patriarchs, a "promised land" that stretches from the Mediterranean Sea to the Euphrates River and from the Sinai Desert in the south to Lebanon in the north. Often, this view leads to an "Israel right or wrong" perspective that is difficult to implement as policy.

Obviously, no matter what stand Bush took on Israel, he risked offending a large number of his religious supporters. But, once again, Bush moved directly to the point. "I am a Christian," he declared, "but I believe with the psalmist that the Lord God of Israel neither slumbers nor sleeps. Understanding my administration should not be difficult. We will speak up for our principles; we will stand up for our friends in the world. And one of the most important friends is the State of Israel." The audience's polite applause indicated that they were not yet convinced.

But the president wasn't done. "At my first meeting of my National Security Council, I told them that a top foreign policy priority of my administration is the safety and the security of Israel. My administration will be steadfast in supporting Israel against terrorism and violence, and in seeking the peace for which all Israelis pray."

It was a general statement, but a reaffirmation of America's continued support for Israel nonetheless. The president would never say such a thing and then let Israel flounder. Surely, in his broad way, he was telling them he was what they wanted him to be: a champion of the State of Israel, a defender against her enemies. Surely it signaled a strengthening of his resolve to stand with America's "important friend." Reassured, the applause offered by the audience became warmer, more sincere.

Bush then turned to the matter of the Middle East as a whole. He was about to issue a noble call for peace, but his words were tinged with such a uniquely American naiveté that some in the audience would remember them with sadness long after the horrors that were five months in the future.

"The Middle East," the president reminded, "is the birthplace of three great religions: Judaism, Christianity, and Islam. Lasting peace in the region must respect the rights of believers in all these faiths. That's common sense. But it is also something more: It is moral sense based upon the deep American commitment to freedom of religion."

American politicians often speak this way. They are idealistic. They dream of a world of equality and freedom, and they assume that other nations do as well. But they also tend to view the world through a uniquely American lens, as though all other nations are somewhere on the road to becoming American. Sometimes they speak as though Thomas Jefferson was not just an American Founding Father but the emperor of a global empire. In his speech to the AJC, Bush sounded very much the same way, for he has just said that peace in the Middle East will come when those in the region share the "deep American commitment to freedom of religion."

It would be nice. Christianity would allow it. Judaism would allow it. But people were not blowing themselves up in Jerusalem shopping centers to bring about the equality of all religions. No, those who were committed to the destruction of Israel believed that the infidel had to die.[49] Did the president understand this? Did he understand that not everything that grows in America can be translated to foreign soil? Did he know the difference between Texas and Tel Aviv?

He soon would.

In just a few short months, he would understand all too well.

Leading the way: With rescue workers at ground zero,
September 14, 2001.

CHAPTER SEVEN

A New Day of Infamy

The Secret Service's code name for Ronald Reagan was "Rawhide." For Jimmy Carter it was "Rabbit." Agents called Bill Clinton "Elvis." They have had two code names for George W. Bush. During the campaign, they called him "Tumbler." Once he took office, he became "Trailblazer."

Today, the word *Trailblazer* will crackle through the airwaves with rare urgency. It is September 11, 2001.

The president is visiting Emma E. Booker Elementary School in Sarasota, Florida. The atmosphere at the school is energized with the odd mixture of excitement and gravity that usually accompanies presidential appearances. Teachers are nervously scurrying their students to appointed positions though the students themselves have gone wooden-legged in awe. The president has arrived. He is at ease, joking, touching a face here, patting a head there.

A few moments before 9:00 A.M., the president is stopped in a hallway by an aide. A plane has hit one of the towers of New York's World Trade Center. The president moves to a private room and converses by phone with National Security Advisor Condoleezza Rice. The crash appears to be an accident, he is told. He continues with his tour.

At 9:04, while Bush is listening to second-graders read, Chief of Staff Andrew Card whispers in his ear that a second plane has struck the other World Trade Center tower. The president's face goes granite, but he continues listening to the students and jokes that they read so well they must be sixth-graders.

He gently extracts himself from the children and huddles with his advisors. There is another conversation with Rice. Bush is to give a speech on education in a few minutes. At 9:30, he enters the school's media center and announces that there has been "an apparent terrorist attack on our country."[1]

"Trailblazer secure. Returning to Air Force One."

The president orders his plane to Washington. Once the wheels are up, the 747 climbs quickly to altitude, decreasing the likelihood of snipers or surface-to-air missiles. This is standard practice, but today the climb is steeper than usual.

Before long, the Secret Service receives information that Air Force One itself is a target. Returning to Washington is too risky. The plane will reroute to Barksdale Air Force Base in Louisiana.[2]

Then it comes: the news that the Pentagon has been hit and that another plane, possibly intended for the White House, has crashed near Pittsburgh.

The president arrives in Louisiana at 12:40 P.M. eastern daylight time. From a general's conference room, he tells

Dick Cheney, who is in a bunker underneath the White House with other cabinet officials, that "it's the faceless coward that attacks."[3]

He makes his first address to the nation. He assures the American people that the government is working, that he is in contact with his leaders and with heads of state around the world. "The resolve of our great nation is being tested," he acknowledges. "But make no mistake: We will show the world that we will pass this test. God bless."[4]

David Frum, who is at this moment in Washington working on the president's speech for later that evening, remembers that the words of the president's first address to the nation were betrayed by the setting: "Air Force bases do not come equipped with television studios, so the president was obliged to record his message in a bare room over a herky-jerky digital connection. He looked and sounded like the hunted, not the hunter."[5]

"Trailblazer moving."

Bush leaves the conference room, hunches down in a camouflaged Humvee, and returns to Air Force One. He talks to Cheney again, who convinces him to fly to Strategic Air Command at Offutt Air Force Base in Nebraska. It is a critical decision. Offutt was designed to be the command center for a response to invasion or nuclear attack. The president going there now makes a clear statement. We are at war. The commander in chief is going to his battle station.

By 3:07 eastern time, as Air Force One is landing at Offutt, the president has spoken to Governor George Pataki and New York City mayor Rudolph Giuliani. "I know your heart is broken and your city is strained," he says, "and anything we can do, let me know."[6]

In Washington, David Frum has just heard from his wife that Barbara Olson, wife of Solicitor General Theodore

Olson, was on the plane that crashed into the Pentagon. Frum's response of faith captures that of so many on this day that it is worth remembering: "I keep a transliteration of the Kaddish, the Jewish prayer for the dead, on my PalmPilot. I stepped out of our little office, retreated to the photocopy room, closed the door, and looked around for something with which to cover my head. I could find nothing, so I pulled my arms out of my jacket, pulled it up and over my head like a shawl, recited the ancient words, and mourned my brave and beautiful friend."[7]

"Trailblazer returning."

After less than ninety minutes at Offutt, the president has decided that his place is in Washington. The *Wall Street Journal* later said this decision showed that the president "could not be frightened away for long, if at all."[8]

"Trailblazer aboard."

From Air Force One Bush calls his wife. "I'm coming home; see you at the White House."[9] He begins working on his prime time speech.

At 8:30 P.M., back in Washington, the president goes on the air. Again, the words are right. "Terrorist attacks can shake the foundations of our biggest buildings, but they cannot touch the foundation of America. These acts shatter steel, but they cannot dent the steel of American resolve." And, for those who grieve, "I pray they will be comforted by a power greater than any of us, spoken through the ages in Psalm 23: 'Even though I walk through the valley of the shadow of death, I fear no evil for You are with me.'"[10]

It helps. America sees her president in the Oval Office and in charge. But the speech does not rise to the magnitude of the occasion. Again, wordsmith Frum writes: "I could imagine Americans switching off their television sets and looking at one another with the same dismay I felt. I could imagine them thinking: Bush was a nice fellow, a perfectly adequate president for a time of peace and quiet; but this was war, real war, and he had given not one indication all day long of readiness for his terrible new responsibilities."[11] Staffers will call Bush's talk the "Awful Office Address."

At 8:35, Bush attends a national security meeting. The discussions, the processing of conflicting reports, continue until 10:21 P.M. The president says goodnight to his staff and joins his wife.

"Trailblazer. Second floor of the residence."

—w—

Earlier that morning, the president's regular habit of reading from Oswald Chambers' *My Utmost for His Highest* would have led him to a very telling passage—how telling, he could not have known at the time. The short reading, entitled "Missionary Munitions," described the model of servant-leadership from the Gospel of John and perhaps portrayed the path the president would have to take in the difficult days ahead: "Ministering as opportunity surrounds us does not mean selecting our surroundings, it means being very selectly God's in any haphazard surroundings which He engineers for us. The characteristics we manifest in our immediate surroundings are indications of what we will be like in other surroundings."[12]

He would indeed soon find himself in haphazard surroundings. The passage continued, even more dramatically: "Towels and dishes and sandals, all the ordinary sordid things of our lives, reveal more quickly than anything what we are made of. It takes God Almighty Incarnate in us to do the meanest duty as it ought to be done." And finally: "We have to go the 'second mile' with God. Some of us get played out in the first ten yards, because God compels us to go where we cannot see the way, and we say, 'I will wait till I get nearer the big crisis.' If we do not do the running steadily in the little ways, we shall do nothing in the crisis."[13]

—⚬—

He had made, however understandably, an unsteady start. As Americans went uneasily to sleep on the night of September 11, they knew their government still stood, but they could not have known much more. Perhaps it was not possible to know. But leadership is not a matter of giving knowledge: It is in the offering of hope, and Bush had not offered convincing hope on this critical day.

On the next day, though, he began to lead. In fact, he began to take the first tentative steps toward becoming Churchillian. In comments to the press made in the Cabinet Room with his security team, Bush defined the nature of the battle. "This will be a monumental struggle of good versus evil," he said, "but good will prevail."[14]

The comment is more important than it may seem. Bush intuitively did what Churchill did. He framed the battle by setting it in moral perspective. Churchill did not say that the battle before the British people was a conflict between England and Germany. He said it was a war between "idolatrous paganism" and "the Christian nations."[15] He defined the conflict in moral terms and, thus, elevated it.

If Bush had simply spoken of 9/11 as a "terrorist act," he would have left Americans believing that the whole matter could be handled by the FBI and local police. Instead, he called the nation to war. He was applying the moral vision that had so transformed his personal life to his nation's collective nightmare. He was beginning to see the challenge clearly now. We are good. Our attackers are evil. To arms. And, he gave hope: "Good will prevail."[16]

He also showed heart. Americans expected competence, but they needed humanity: for the president to grieve as they were grieving. On September 13, Bush took a few questions from reporters. One of them asked, "What is in your heart?" Tears formed in his eyes, and his lips quivered. Haltingly, he said, "I think about the families, the children. I am a loving guy, and I am also someone, however, who has got a job to do—and I intend to do it."[17] When the nation heard it, they felt he was one of them.

It was on the next day, though, that Bush stepped into his own. It is not insignificant that it happened in a church. During the memorial service at the National Cathedral, he gave a speech in which he was, perhaps for the first time in office, both theological and poetic. Americans had gathered in "the middle hour" of their grief, he said, and while the nation did not have the "distance of history," she did have a "responsibility to history...to answer these attacks and rid the world of evil." He was approaching Churchill again, morally defining the battle, making the coming sacrifices worth the price. "This nation is peaceful," he assured, "but fierce when stirred to anger." Here he neared Roosevelt, warning the world of America's "righteous wrath." And a little bit of Patton: "This conflict was begun on the timing and terms of others. It will end in a way, and at an hour, of our choosing."[18]

He then began to define a theology fit for the nation's suffering. "This world," he intoned, "is of moral design. Grief and tragedy and hatred are only for a time. Goodness, remembrance, and love have no end. And the Lord of life holds all who die, and all who mourn." Evil will pass, he was saying, but the good is eternal. This was the world-view, though. The pastoral counsel came next: "It is said that adversity introduces us to ourselves. This is true of a nation as well."[19] And what kind of nation was America finding herself to be? The kind that makes heroes: the priest who died giving last rites, the man who stayed in the towers with his paraplegic friend, the firefighters who climbed to their deaths.

America is good, then, but good nations are not "spared from suffering." Instead, we have suffered precisely "because we are freedom's home and defender. And the commitment of our fathers is now the calling of our time."[20] We are destined for this. It is the price we pay for being good. It is worth the fight.

And we will not be alone: "As we have been assured, neither death nor life, nor angels nor principalities nor power, nor things present nor things to come, nor height nor depth, can separate us from God's love. May He bless the souls of the departed. May He comfort our own. And may He always guide our country. God bless America."[21]

It was, some said, the best speech of his life. Bush seemed to sense it, too. He was making language part of the national arsenal, learning the power of a president to impart the moral sense to a nation in crisis. And he was feeling the strength that comes from believing oneself destined.

Immediately after the service, he flew to New York for the first time since the attacks. With Mayor Giuliani and Governor Pataki at his side, he toured ground zero. The crowds inspired him. They waved flags and handwritten signs of encouragement while chanting "USA! USA!"

Then came a scene no advance team could have scripted. While Bush was touring the wreckage, rescue workers began to gather around him. Wanting to hear him speak, someone handed him a megaphone. He looked like he was ready, but he paused when he realized he could not be seen by most of the crowd.

A retired fireman named Bill Beckwith mounted a destroyed fire truck nearby to see if it would hold the president. It would. Beckwith helped Bush up, and then found he could not step down because Bush had his arm around him and was not moving it. Bush began to speak, but he sounded garbled through the megaphone. Someone shouted, "We can't hear you." Seizing the moment, Bush pulled the megaphone away from his mouth and shouted, "Well, I can hear you." There were cheers. Then he hesitated, as though reflecting on the meaning of his own words. "I can hear you," he said again. "The rest of the world hears you. And the people who knocked these buildings down will hear all of us soon." The crowd got it—the meaning of the moment, the fact that Bush was stepping out into his own, the promise that the suffering would be avenged—and they erupted in joyous chant: "USA! USA! USA!"[22]

More than a few commentators have said that from this day Bush was never the same. His speeches improved. He spoke more boldly of his faith. His confidence became infectious.

He knew it was happening, too. A writer commented to him that he had slashed lines from a major speech that would surely have made the newspaper headlines. Bush shook his head and replied, "The headline is: Bush leads."[23]

—⁂—

He was feeling new power, and he was about to need it. Six days after the tragedy of September 11, he made a speech at the Islamic Center of Washington that would incite more controversy than anything he had yet said in office. To a largely Muslim audience, Bush said, "Islam is peace…When we think of Islam, we think of a faith that brings comfort to a billion people around the world. Billions of people find comfort and solace and peace. And that's made brothers and sisters out of every race."[24]

His intent was good. He was trying to separate terrorism from Islam. He wanted the nearly one and one-half billion Muslims in the world to know that the steps he was about to take were not against their faith but against those who used their faith as a pretext for violence. He also knew that to deal effectively with more radical Muslim countries like Afghanistan he would need favor with the moderate ones like Jordan and Turkey.

Yet the words "Islam is peace" rang hollow with many Americans just days after 9/11. They also seemed to contradict what Americans saw when they looked out at the world. In Nigeria, Sudan, Indonesia, Israel, Afghanistan, Pakistan, Iraq, India, and, of course, now the United States, many Muslims seemed to be less than peaceful. Islam did not appear to be what the president said: a religion that "made brothers and sisters of every race." There was a storm of criticism from the Religious Right following Bush's remarks. As one missionary/author asked, referring to the date of the president's speech, "We can survive 9/11, but can we survive 9/17?"[25]

Bush's speech to the nation three days later incited his critics even more. In his September 20 address to a joint session of Congress, he said, "The terrorists practice a fringe form of Islamic extremism that has been rejected by Muslim scholars and the vast majority of Muslim clerics, a fringe movement that perverts the peaceful teachings of Islam."[26]

This time, though, it was not just Bush's words that rankled some critics. Sitting in the gallery with Laura Bush during the speech was Hamza Yusuf. He was there by presidential invitation. Two days before September 11, Yusuf had spoken in support of Sheikh Omar Abdel-Rahman, the blind Muslim cleric who inspired the first attempt to blow up the World Trade Center in 1993. "This country is facing a terrible fate," Yusuf had mysteriously prophesied. "The reason for that is that this country stands condemned. It stands condemned like Europe stood condemned...after conquering the Muslim Lands."[27] More than one observer wondered why a man of such opinions should be invited to sit in the gallery during a presidential speech intended to announce a campaign against terrorists.

Bush was attempting to be presidential—to model his nation's commitment to religious freedom and tolerance—but his statements regarding Islam continued to confuse some Americans and concern others. On the one hand, he asserted, as he did in his September 17 speech, that most American Muslims "love this country as much as I do." On the other hand, he used words like *crusade* to describe the war on terror, a term so laden with history as to be unique in its power to offend the Muslim world.[28] Bush was sounding an uncertain trumpet, and some observers could not decide whether this was due to his own acknowledged lack of theological sophistication or the White House's attempt to make the difficult distinction between Islam and Islamic fundamentalism.

Some thought there was a more political explanation. Already there had been reports, widely accepted in the Bush administration, that Muslims tipped the balance in the 2000 election. The Tampa Bay Islamic Center, for example, had reported that of the fifty thousand Muslims who voted in Florida, 88 percent voted for Bush.[29] That would be forty-four thousand votes, clearly the deciding factor in Florida, which was, in turn, the deciding state in the nation. While seeking to reassure Muslims worldwide and win them as allies in the war on terrorism, Bush may also have been safeguarding his hold on the Muslim vote in the United States. If true, it was a tricky balancing act given his strong support from the Religious Right, and it was about to become even more difficult.

—∞—

On November 16, NBC News aired remarks by evangelist Franklin Graham that threatened to both inflame the Muslim world and distance Bush from his religious base. The son of Billy Graham, Franklin had already weathered charges of religious bigotry after he concluded his prayer at Bush's inauguration with the words, "We pray this in the name of the Father, and of the Son, the Lord Jesus Christ, and of the Holy Spirit." Many non-Christian and nonreligious Americans were offended, but Graham was unrepentant. "I'm a minister of the Gospel of the Lord Jesus Christ," he told the *Washington Post*. "That's who I am. What I am."[30] When Bush showed public support for Graham, the matter quickly died out.

On the issue of Islam, however, Bush and Graham were not of the same mind. Graham told one interviewer that Islam is "wicked, violent and not of the same god."[31] "I don't believe this is a wonderful, peaceful religion," the minister later told NBC. "When you read the Quran and you read the verses from the Quran, it instructs the killing of the infidel, for those that are non-Muslim...It wasn't Methodists flying into those buildings, it wasn't Lutherans. It was an attack on this country by people of the Islamic faith."[32]

In a piece written for the *Wall Street Journal*, Graham defended his views. "I do not believe Muslims are evil people because of their faith," he insisted. "But I decry the evil that has been done in the name of Islam, or any other faith— including Christianity. I agree with President Bush that as a country we are at war with terrorists, not with Islam. But as a minister, not a politician, I believe it is my responsibility to speak out against the terrible deeds that are committed as a result of Islamic teaching."[33]

Graham's comments carried weight because of his appearance at Bush's inaugural, because he was the son of the world's most famous evangelist, and because his ministry, Samaritan's Purse, had "provided more relief to Muslim people than to any other group in the world."[34] Clearly, he was not speaking from the fringe of Christian opinion, and his comments were so widely circulated that the White House issued a statement reiterating that President Bush "views Islam as a religion that preaches peace."[35]

Graham's clarification did little to quell the storm of controversy, and over the months that followed, other leaders of the Religious Right echoed his concerns about Islam. Jerry Falwell declared on CBS's *60 Minutes* that "Muhammad was a terrorist...a violent man, a man of war."[36] On *The 700 Club*, Pat Robertson said, "Adolf Hitler was bad, but what the Muslims want to do to the Jews is worse."[37]

In remarks to reporters as he began a meeting with U.N. Secretary General Kofi Annan, Bush specifically addressed these charges. "Some of the comments that have been uttered about Islam do not reflect the sentiments of my government or the sentiments of most Americans," he said. "By far, the vast majority of the American citizens respect the Islamic people and the Muslim faith. After all, there are millions of peace-loving Muslim Americans. Ours is a country based upon tolerance...and we're not going to let the war on terror or terrorists cause us to change our values."[38]

To Bush's credit, it is likely that his position on Islam prevented stronger backlash against Muslims in the wake of 9/11. In the first days after the tragedy, there had been violence against both Muslims and those mistakenly thought to be Muslim. In one state, Sikh Hindus were beaten because they were thought to be Muslims. In another state, youths vandalized a synagogue thinking that it was the same thing as a mosque. Genuine Muslims, of course, suffered abuse as well. Bush's stand for tolerance, his distinguishing between Islam and terrorism, and his campaign to court favor with Muslims at home and abroad, whatever its motivations, was probably responsible for safeguarding the well-being, if not the lives, of many Muslims worldwide.

This crisis in defining the nature of Islam also answered one of the strongest criticisms of Bush: that he was a pawn of preachers. For Bush to oppose the views of the leading religious broadcasters in the country meant he risked alienating the core of his political base. It also meant he risked questions from members of his own faith about whether he believed in the preeminence of Christianity. Yet he did not cave in. He spoke of tolerance, of the will of an American majority, and of the good to be found in Islam. He chose to be president of a democracy rather than the "preacher in chief" his critics thought him to be—and that some on the Right wanted him to be.

Bush passed the test that many in the nonreligious American majority needed to see him pass. He could hold the line with preachers of his faith, he could submit his beliefs to democratic principles, and he could be the president of all the people, not just the president of the born again. His approval ratings soared in confirmation.

—⁂—

Shortly after the tragedies of September 11, Bush began defining a new American military doctrine. In doing so, he also launched a heated theological debate. In his September 20 address to Congress, the president announced that nations harboring terrorists "will hand over the terrorists, or they will share in their fate."[39] This became the basis for the "Bush doctrine" that would, in turn, become the rationale for America's incursions into Afghanistan and Iraq. Simply stated, to protect herself from international terrorism, the United States would now deem "preemptive strikes" and invasion of "terrorist-harboring nations" as legitimate uses of her power.

Throughout American history, presidents had regularly articulated the nation's defense posture in public speeches. From the Monroe Doctrine of America's early decades to Teddy Roosevelt's "gunboat diplomacy," from the "isolationism" of the early twentieth century to the containment policy of the Cold War years, presidents had often defined the extent of the country's willingness to exercise military might.

Bush now joined their ranks, but his insistence that America had the right to invade sovereign nations whenever she felt threatened raised questions. Does the United States have a responsibility to provide evidence for her conclusions about the presence of terrorists in other nations? How accountable is the United States to the United Nations? What kind of warning should targeted nations receive? What responsibility do American forces have for rebuilding an invaded nation?

Given Bush's religious orientation, many expected that the administration's answers to these questions would be drawn from the theology that had guided Christians in their thinking about war for centuries: the "Just War" theory. First formulated by St. Augustine in his classic *The City of God*, the Just War theory was an attempt to answer the questions of early Christians about the ethics of fighting in the wars of the Roman Empire: "When is it permissible to wage war, *jus in bello*?" and "What are the limitations on the ways we wage war, *jus ad bellum*?"

Augustine taught that there are four primary conditions that must be met for a war to be morally justified. The first is proper authority. As he put it, "The natural order, which is suited to the peace of moral things, requires that the authority and deliberation for undertaking war be under the control of a leader."[40] Augustine's second requirement is proper cause. He specifically ruled out as justifications for war such causes as "the desire for harming, the cruelty of revenge, the restless and implacable mind, the savageness of revolting, and the lust for dominating." Augustine saw war as a tragic necessity, and he admonished rulers to "let necessity slay the warring foe, not your will."[41]

The third of Augustine's principles requires that there be a reasonable chance of success. Even if a nation has good reason to wage war, it must not send young men to their deaths without an attainable goal: Human life is too sacred to waste, he argued. Finally, Augustine insisted on the condition of proportionality. In waging a war, he argued, the authorities must make sure that the harm caused by their response to aggression does not exceed the harm caused by the aggression itself.

Though the Bush administration did not invoke the Just War theory at first, much of the debate about the invasions of Afghanistan and Iraq outside the administration clearly centered on Augustine's ideas. For example, in a widely cited article, former President Jimmy Carter expressed his opposition to the Bush doctrine on a Just War basis: "As a Christian and as a president who was severely provoked by international crises, I became thoroughly familiar with the principles of a Just War, and it is clear that a substantially unilateral attack on Iraq does not meet these standards."[42]

Similarly, the president of Chicago Theological Seminary, Susan Thistlethwaite, wrote in the *Chicago Tribune*, "No part of Just War theory supports a first-strike option...Augustine wanted to know if Christians could resist barbarians. If the United States adopts and acts on a first-strike option, then it is Americans who have become the barbarians. We will have learned nothing from 1,500 years of moral reasoning."[43]

Not surprisingly, Bush's supporters cited the same theory. Robert P. George, the McCormick Professor of Jurisprudence at Princeton University, told the *National Review*, "The just-war theory is a common patrimony of Catholic, Protestant, and Orthodox Christians. Moreover, the teachings of Jewish tradition on war and peace are closely in line with it." As a result, he said, "The use of military force against terrorist networks and regimes abetting their crimes is certainly justifiable...according to Just War principles."[44]

Realizing the power of the Just War argument, the Bush administration eventually began using Augustine's conditions to make the case for war. Jim Nicholson, the U.S. ambassador to the Holy See, invited economist and Catholic lay-theologian Michael Novak to Rome to give a lecture in a series sponsored by the embassy on the evening of February 10, 2003. Novak argued that the invasion of Iraq "comes under traditional just-war doctrine, for this war is a lawful conclusion to the just war fought and swiftly won in February, 1991."[45] His comments were widely circulated and regularly cited by the president's apologists in the popular media.

Spokesmen for the administration picked up the language of the Just War theory, and some of Bush's aides began urging him to do the same. The suggestion met with little success. It is typical of Bush. He eschews the theoretical and prefers the simple expressions that lead to action rather than the complex theories that he thinks will lead to perpetual debate. In this case, he preferred to call Saddam an "evildoer." This, for him, is the case for war. Saddam is evil. He threatens good people. Evildoers have no legitimacy. Removing Saddam is a moral act. Case closed. It is a case built from the psalms of David rather than the ruminations of Augustine.

It may also be a case rooted in his own personal sense of destiny. As Norman Podhoretz, editor of the conservative Jewish journal *Commentary* and a senior fellow at the Hudson Institute, explained, "One hears that Bush...feels that there was a purpose behind his election all along: as a born-again Christian, it is said, he believes he was chosen by God to eradicate the evil of terrorism from the world. I think it is a plausible rumor, and I would even guess that in his heart of hearts, Bush identifies more in this respect with Ronald Reagan—the president who rid the world of the 'evil empire'—than with his own father, who never finished the job he started in taking on Saddam Hussein."[46]

Podhoretz's guess that George W. is motivated by his father's failure may miss the mark, but the president may actually be motivated by another matter related to his father. Bush has not forgotten that Saddam Hussein attempted to assassinate his father. In September of 2002, while Bush was embroiled in conflict with the Senate over matters of "homeland security," Bush completed a comment to reporters on the importance of removing Saddam Hussein by adding, "After all, this is the guy who tried to kill my dad."[47]

It is a sentimental reflection that seems almost touchingly out of place in the hard-hitting world of presidential politics. Yet, it is vitally revealing of who George W. Bush is. He is willing to cite in partial justification for mobilizing the world's mightiest military force against one of this generation's worst tyrants that the villain tried to kill his father. For him, the personal and the public are intertwined, as are public policy and personal morality. This, again, is Bush the relational, the man who "relates" to truth rather than reasons himself to it.

Clearly, a presidential administration is more than one man, one personality, or one intellectual type. But the Bush administration does deeply reflect its leader, and this means that policy, even in military matters, will be processed in terms of the personal, in terms of the moral, and in terms of a sense of divine purpose that propels the present to meet the challenges of its time.

Down to earth: The president very much at home on his
South Texas ranch, August 9, 2002.

CHAPTER EIGHT

Bush Unbound

We live in an age that insists upon narrowly defined categories, and we expect reality to fit neatly within them. Everything must have its type, its genre, its precise position on the rightly labeled shelf. This may be due to our media-saturated, market-defined, computer-scanned culture, or it may be a kind of laziness that makes us search for symbols to save us from having to think. Whatever the reason, it can make us like the overworked librarian who simply discards books for which she has no preexisting label.

The danger is that we will discard the amorphous qualities that make us human. Or we will degrade them. Our need to fit reality into a grid of reference forces us to cut away at the human spirit in order to pack the human being in the box of our definitions. It makes the world uniform, inaccurate, and—dull. It drives away the mystery, the fun, and, often, the meaning.

This very insistence on type and label characterizes much that is said of George W. Bush. Let us reduce him to the minimum, pin a label on him, and work all that he says and does into the narrative of our characterizations. This makes our work easier and frees us from having to consider the nuances, the contradictions, and the naturally human texture of his life. But it also leaves us with little that is real.

He is, for example a cowboy-hat-wearing Texan who does not read much, is not very articulate, and is no one's idea of an intellectual. This makes him the Bubba-type: with all the low-brow, Southern cracker, "rifle-in-the-gun-rack-of-the-pickup-truck" image that label evokes. It puts a "handle" on him, makes him easy to slot and easy to hate.

However, he is also an Ivy League product whose administration is the most racially diverse in American history and who in mid-2003 traveled to Africa to acknowledge the sin of slavery.[1] In fact, he has used the occasion to honor the Civil Rights movement: "By a plan known only to Providence, the stolen sons and daughters of Africa helped to awaken the conscience of America. The very people traded into slavery helped to set America free."[2]

Moreover, his black National Security Advisor has said that slavery is the "birth defect" in American history.[3] He agrees. He spends more time meeting with black ministers like T. D. Jakes, Tony Evans, and Kirbyjon Caldwell and is as open to their input as any president in recent memory. And this is despite the fact that when a video greeting by Bush was played at a T. D. Jakes' women's conference, many of the eighty-thousand-strong, primarily black audience booed him.

The challenge of Bush is that he does not play the role

assigned to him. He is always surprising us. He eludes our definitions and insists on being his own man. Perhaps if, as he says, his faith frees him, it frees him to be more human and thus more indefinable than both psychoanalysis and political punditry would prefer.

—⁓—

Consider this scene: It is the White House Press Correspondents Dinner in early May of 2002. The press corps, with their spouses and dates, are all in attendance at the elegant affair, as are President and Mrs. Bush. And there is another invitee, one who seems a bit out of place. His hair is beyond shoulder-length, his colorful tattoos fill his arms and crawl up his neck, and his years of substance abuse have left him with a look on his face that crosses deer-caught-in-headlights with irritated owl.

His name is Ozzy Osbourne—the rocker of biting-the-heads-off-of-bats fame, of language-so-bad-that-MTV-bleeps-every-other-word fame.

The president rises to make a few remarks. Turning to Mr. Osbourne, he says, "The thing about Ozzy is, he's made a lot of big hit recordings: 'Party With the Animals,' 'Sabbath Bloody Sabbath,' 'Facing Hell,' 'Black Skies' and 'Bloodbath in Paradise.'"[4]

The audience is taken aback. They are not sure what is coming next, and they are somewhat surprised that this notoriously Christian and country-music president can name those songs.

Bush, of course, is smirking. While the audience chuckles, he says, "Ozzy, my mom loves your stuff."[5] The place erupts with laughter.

Immediately after the dinner, some conservatives and religious leaders protest that the president has welcomed such a cultural villain into the hallowed halls. The White House has no comment except to say that a good time was had by all.

What type is the president now? What category can we fit him into?

Now, consider this: Bush is so conservative in style and politics his friends in the sixties said he belonged to their parents' generation. Yet his primary ally on the world scene is the leader of the British Labor Party, Tony Blair. Virtually alone, they stood together in support of the invasion of Iraq, and they have opened up a new chapter in Anglo-American relations.

At the foundation of their friendship is faith. Blair was raised by an atheist father and a mother who went to church only occasionally. At Oxford, he became a Christian of the long-haired, guitar-playing variety and later joined the Christian Socialist movement then spreading through Europe. He pioneered his New Labor movement on a foundation of faith, distinguishing it from Old Labor, which was notoriously atheistic.

Still, he was careful about wrapping politics in religious garb. "I can't stand politicians who wear God on their sleeves," he wrote in 1996. "I do not pretend to be any better or less selfish than anyone else; I do not believe that Christians should only vote Labor." He also described prayer as "a source of solace," the Gospels as "a most extraordinary expression of sensitive human values," and Jesus as a "modernizer."[6]

And George W. Bush, the conservative millionaire businessman, is the friend of this ex-hippie Labor leader. They have shared Scripture together, prayed together, and discussed the morality of policy on walks at Camp David. Clearly, faith trumps politics in their relationship.

So, which of the Bush-types is this?

And then: In 1994, while campaigning for governor, Bush expressed his support for a sodomy law that criminalized homosexuality. He called it "a symbolic gesture of traditional values."[7]

It should be said, too, that his conservative Christianity brands homosexual conduct a sin, and his philosophy of culture regards it as destructive of a healthy society.

Yet, on April 9, 2001, just months after taking office, Bush appointed an openly gay man, Scott H. Evertz, as director of the Office of National AIDS Policy. Later, he appointed another homosexual man, Michael Guest, as U.S. ambassador to Romania.[8]

On what shelf do we put this version of the president?

—m—

The "profiling" of Bush fails us. The truth is much simpler and much more complex at the same time. He is a man of faith feeling his way along the dimly lit path of religiously responsible politics. He has no blueprint, no modern handbook for being both president and Christian, conservative, compassionate, fully human, and engaged in life all at the same time. Yet, he has assumptions laid upon him that are rooted more in myths about religion than in anything he has said or done.

Chief among the fears inspired by a conservative Christian in the White House is that he will hasten the coming of Armageddon. This is particularly a concern among the non-Christian and the nonreligious—those forced to stand outside the fold and listen to Christian end-of-history scenarios that shame the wildest science fiction. Not all Christians hold such views, though, and those who don't resent having the assumption laid on them.

The myth goes something like this: All Bible-thumpers believe that history will end with a cataclysmic battle on a plain called Armageddon just north of Jerusalem, and Bible-thumping politicians see it as their duty to bring this battle to pass. This fear was first inspired by Reagan's ruminations on the End Times and has gained new currency with the popularity of the Left Behind series of novels in America.

Even his critics admit that this is a misrepresentation of both Bush and his staff. Journalist Christopher Hitchens has written, "Neither Gerson nor Rove has anything to do with 'end time' or 'premillennial' Christianity, and neither believes that an intense military tussle with Satan is soon to take place at Armageddon. This is an often circulated slander against them, and against Bush, too."[9]

Such assumptions about religion and the religious make suspect the simplest statements. On May 8, 1999, John Ashcroft, the future attorney general, was awarded an honorary doctorate by Bob Jones University. In a short speech of thanks, Ashcroft mentioned that during the American Revolution, correspondence from the colonies to George III included the statement "We have no king but Jesus." He went on to make comparisons between a "culture that has no king but Caesar, no standard but the civil authority, and a culture that has no king but Jesus, no standard but the eternal authority."[10]

The three-minute speech caused a firestorm of controversy. Critics accused Ashcroft of advocating a theocracy and trouncing the First Amendment. Even four years later, Christopher Hitchens rebuked Ashcroft by saying, "We have no king at all, and we have no state church, or official religion, and that's that. It's also supposed to be the essential difference between ourselves and the homicidal fundamentalists."[11]

However, Ashcroft was simply recalling the intent of the Founding Fathers. And he was right. Correspondence with King George did include the phrase "No king but Jesus," and it so resonated with the colonists that militiamen chanted it as they marched into battle. The fear of such historical references arises from the belief that all religious-types in politics want a theocracy. Not the soft-spoken Ashcroft, though. In the text of an earlier speech released by the White House to address the controversy, Ashcroft stated, "We must embrace the power of faith, but we must never confuse politics and piety. For me, may I say that it is against my religion to impose my religion."[12]

This fear of the religious impetus in politics is often rooted in oversimplification. For example, when Bush was once asked what people could pray for in the wake of 9/11, he said, "That there's a shield of protection, so that if the vile ones try to hit us again, that we've done everything we can, physically, and that there is a spiritual shield that protects the country."[13] One commentator replied, "My God, is that all he's relying on, a shield of prayer?"

Yet Bush's statement came months after he had launched the war in Afghanistan and as he was planning the invasion of Iraq. He does not believe in prayer *or* missiles, the spiritual *or* the natural. He believes they are both intertwined, that the visible and the invisible parallel, which is simply the "mere Christianity" of the ages. His critics on religious matters, not understanding this, want to paint him as hypermystical.

What confuses some is the earthly nature of Bush's spirituality. He has not grown in his faith by pondering theological problems or meditating on mystical abstractions. He has grown by watching his heroes, listening to stories, and learning of the heavenly through earthly example.

Characteristically, he sees a symbol for the power of sin in the way scrub brush chokes out good plant growth on his ranch. He loves the psalms where spiritual truth is often expressed in terms of nature: The heavens pour forth speech, trees sing for joy, and the seas contain God's "wonders in the deep."

This spiritual earthiness is the foundation of Bush's unique friendship with James Robison. Bush and preachers are not naturally a good fit. He has surely heard the jokes: that a man-eating lion would die of starvation at a preacher's convention, that there are actually three genders—men, women, and preachers. They illustrate the point that ministers are not usually models of masculinity—that manliness is often in short supply among the clergy.

Robison is different. A tall, muscular Texan, Robison is a man's man. His speech is straight and unflowery, delivered with a visceral passion and physicality that draws his listeners in. He hunts, fishes, loves sports, and is at home in the outdoors. This is the common language he shares with Bush. The two have prayed together while hiking Bush's ranch or talked about faith, gun in hand, while waiting for game to approach.[14] Sports and nature provide the metaphor for the spiritual truths the two men share. Here again is another seeming Bush contradiction: His earthiness is the key to his spirituality, the visible is the gateway to his understanding of the invisible.

It must be said that a good deal of the criticism of Bush's faith comes from the belief that he is simpleminded. This springs from the Marxist perspective that "religion is the opiate of the people." Religion dulls the faculties of the dullard. In Bush's case, the assumption is that he's a simpleminded man who clings to unexamined truths and makes them policy by an odd mixture of charm and arrogance.

Yet this questioning of Bush's intelligence is clearly overdone. Any other man introduced as a graduate of Yale and Harvard who made millions of dollars in business, who was a two-term state governor, and who became president of the United States would not be thought stupid, sight unseen.

Moreover, the question seems to deny the existence of various types of intelligence. Decades ago, educators spoke in terms of one kind of intelligence: the literary, abstract-thought-oriented, philosophical variety. Now, research has shown what experience had long revealed: There are different types of intelligence. There is the kind described above, and there is also the mechanical type, known by the boy in school who does poorly at "book-learning" but who can "fix anything." He is not stupid. He just has one type of intelligence, the type most schooling does not reward.

Among the many varieties of intelligence is the one Bush seems to possess: social, intuitive, visceral. It is the relational intelligence of the man who feels his way to truth, learns from people rather than books, and takes what he learns almost permanently into memory. A friend once said that Bush must have known the names of one thousand of the four thousand students at Yale in his day.[15] His memory is often lauded, but it is memory tied to people, to relationships, and to feeling.

Tony Blair has no patience for the view that Bush is unintelligent. It's all "complete bull," he says, "just nonsense. He is highly intelligent, and it's not clotted by so many nuances that the meaning is obscured."[16] Lee Atwater agreed. Speaking of Bush's ability to grasp the mathematics of a campaign, Atwater said, "He was the smartest guy around."[17]

Moreover, Bush's assistant in the late 1980s told the *Atlanta Constitution and Journal*, "When I was working for George W. in '87…I'd bring in his campaign itinerary and stacks of material I'd already sorted through. He did not want excessive detail. And by noon, three quarters of the stuff would be in the trash can, and when he'd go for his noon jog, I'd be picking the stuff out of the trash can and I'd think, 'You couldn't have read this.' But he had, and picked out the facts and put it somewhere in his mind and moved on."[18]

It is actually this very relational type of intelligence that sometimes gets him in trouble. He is prone to overstate because he feels connected to a group, and then speaks about them in generalizations. He once said, "America believes deeply that everybody has worth, everybody matters, everybody was created by the Almighty."[19] Clearly, this latter phrase is not true of all Americans, but Bush believes it himself, feels the relational connect with Americans, and expresses it as though speaking for "his people." It is the downside of his brand of intelligence.

There is an upside, though. He is quick witted, particularly when verbally sparring with people. Again, the relational brings out the best in him. He once jabbed at reporters during his presidential campaign by saying, "I don't read half of what you write." Undaunted, a reporter shot back, "We don't listen to half of what you say." "That's apparent," Bush replied calmly, "in the other half of what I read."[20]

He is also sophomorically playful. If anyone is throwing food on Air Force One, it is likely to be the president. Of all the Latin he might have remembered from his school days, the phrase he summons most is *ubi ubi sub ubi*. It is a pun, which loosely translates, "Where, oh where, is your underwear?" Reporters have caught the nation's chief executive making faces through his napkin and hiding a staffer's pen or notebook while feigning innocence. It is endearing and human, but it feeds the low-intelligence myth.

This myth leads observers to credit anyone but Bush for his accomplishments. One of the enduring assumptions about Bush's rise to prominence is that whatever he does not owe to his father, he owes to his chief strategist, Karl Rove, who is credited with making his boss "presidential." He is heralded as one of the finest American political strategists since Lee Atwater. He has even been called "Bush's Brain."[21] There is little doubt that Rove is brilliant, driven, and effective. But according to longtime friend Richard Land, "George W. Bush has influenced Karl Rove far more than Karl Rove has influenced George W. Bush."[22] Concurring, James Robison has insisted that "Rove knows that only too well."[23]

The assumption that Bush's faith is inherently lowbrow can lead to an underestimating of his policies. This seems to be the case in the opposition to his push for funding of faith-based initiatives. Critics accuse him of forcing his religion on the underprivileged or seeking to fund his favorite Christian concerns. The fact is that a solid body of research supports the role of faith in healing and restoration, though this is rarely given merit in the belief that faith-based initiatives are inspired by Bush's faith alone.

Before he resigned as head of the Office of Faith-Based Initiatives, John DiIulio wrote an article for the *Weekly Standard* citing "over 500 scientifically sound studies in which the 'faith factor' was associated with results ranging from reductions in hypertension, depression, and suicide to lower rates of drug abuse, educational failure, nonmarital teenage childbearing, and criminal behavior." He also explained that some "50 empirical studies report that religious influences and institutions reduce violence and delinquency."[24]

DiIulio mentioned as well the unusual decision on then Governor Bush's part to turn a Texas prison over to Charles Colson's ministry, Prison Fellowship. An independent six-year study reported that "two years after release, inmates who completed the 22-month program (16 months in prison plus 6 months of post-release care) were less likely to be rearrested than otherwise comparable inmates who did not participate in the program. Indeed, only 8 percent of the Prison Fellowship program graduates, versus 20 percent of the matched comparison group, were incarcerated within two years after being released."[25]

Clearly, the assumption on the part of Bush's critics that faith is more bias than science prevents them from examining faith-based policies on their own merits. Though religion cannot be scientifically verified, religion's results sometimes can be.

Similarly, assumptions about Bush's religious views often lead to conjecture about his policies toward Israel. Because he is a conservative Christian, some take it as automatic that he is unreservedly pro-Israel. Indeed, Ariel Sharon has spoken of the "deep friendship" and "special closeness" Israel enjoys with the Bush administration. Thomas Neumann, executive director of the Jewish Institute for National Security Affairs, has said, "This is the best administration for Israel since Harry Truman [who first recognized an independent Israel]."[26]

Bush has indeed shown solid support for Israel, but not because he is moved to do so by theology. He believes Israel is a loyal friend, an island of democracy in the Middle East, and a nation with an historic right to exist. Yet, in 2003, Bush helped engineer a "road map to peace" that, if successful, will speed the establishment of an independent Palestinian state on an equal footing with Israel. He invited

Palestinian prime minister Mahmoud Abbas to the White House, a move *BBC News* described as "the first time a Palestinian leader has been given the red carpet treatment during the Bush presidency."[27] Strong supporters of Israel on the Religious and non–Religious Right in America are deeply concerned at Bush's pragmatism. They are not alone. On many issues, Bush is less doctrinaire than his faith would make him appear, and this too is part of the mystery of George W. Bush.

—⁂—

To charges of religious extremism and a lowbrow religion must be added the assumed hypocrisy of Bush's statements on morality. It is a shot that can be fired at almost any figure who invokes the moral implications of faith.

It is often implied that unless a man is morally pure and has been since birth, he has no license to call for moral behavior. This would leave all preaching to angels. The reality is that no one is better equipped to speak to the devastation of immorality like the formerly immoral. Bush is among them.

Conservative commentator Tucker Carlson has described Bush as "a grizzled veteran of the sexual revolution."[28] It may be an overstatement, but it does make the point that, as Bush has said, "When I was young and irresponsible, I was young and irresponsible."[29] Having lived rich and single in a morally experimental age, Bush experimented. It is not hard to imagine the possibilities.

Faith brought moral renovation to Bush's life. It did not happen all at once, but over time he stopped drinking, using tobacco, and raging angrily at his enemies. Moreover, his former excesses saddened him, and he made amends when he could.

An example: In 1986, while he was still learning how to wear his new Christian life, Bush saw Al Hunt of the *Wall Street Journal* in a Dallas restaurant. In an April edition of *Washingtonian* magazine, Hunt had predicted Jack Kemp would win the GOP ticket over Vice President Bush, a statement that infuriated the candidate's son. George W. strode over to Hunt in the restaurant, swore vilely at him in front of his wife and four-year-old child, and said, "I saw what you wrote. We're not going to forget this."[30]

Ten years later, Bill Minutaglio mentioned the incident to Bush while interviewing him for his book, *First Son*. Bush at first could not remember the details, but when Minutaglio recounted Hunt's version of the meeting in Dallas, Bush became reflective. Two weeks later, he called Hunt and apologized. Asked why after a decade he made amends, Bush said, "I heard he was angry about it, and it began to weigh heavy on my mind. I would have done it earlier had I realized I had offended him." He then added, "There's no excuse for me offending him in front of his child...I regret that."[31]

Having transgressed, he knows the power of transgression and urges the young to avoid it. Speaking in support of sexual abstinence for teens and an organization that teaches it, he once said, "Across America, under a program called True Love Waits, nearly a million teens have pledged themselves to abstain from sex until marriage. Our teenagers feel the pressures of complex times, but also the upward pull of a better nature."[32] It is this very "upward pull" he has yielded to in his own soul and that he inspires others to know.

Still, his critics charge, although he is not a hypocrite for having sinned and then called for holiness, they believe he should see about imparting some of his conservative values to his own daughters. Tales of under-age drinking and fake

IDs have been widely reported.[33] Since the twins went to college and began rubbing elbows with celebrities, accounts of marijuana use have begun to surface as well.[34] Clearly, Bush has work to do at home.

Yet, if a man's message is to be voided by the conduct of his children, Winston Churchill should be taken from his pedestal, many preachers would have to resign, and more than a few of Bush's critics would have to reexamine their line of work. Truth is not diminished by the inadequacies of those who preach it. Nor is it altered by the failure of children to absorb their parents' message. Truth is confirmed, however, in the power of a changed life, and Bush models this as few other presidents in American history.

Bush friend James Robison puts it this way: "Actions always speak much louder than words. A changed life speaks more forcefully and clearly than a hundred sermons. George W. Bush is a changed man—a change made obvious, not so much by extreme and sinful expressions of the past, but because he was considered by most a typical all-American guy, a good ol' boy, a baby boomer, successful, fun-loving, a sports enthusiast and outdoors type. By his own admission he was drinking too much and was pretty well absorbed by his own interests.

"The great undeniable change in George W. Bush is revealed in his total commitment to help his country preserve freedom's blessing, to feel compassion for those who suffer, his love for God, his faith, and his desire for peace around the world.

"Suddenly, as a result of his faith commitment, the well-being of others became the priority directing his life and future. His own comfort and aversion to public life in the political arena were lost by the consuming desire to make a positive difference through principled leadership. In personal

confession and public acknowledgment during one presidential debate, George W. Bush shared his belief that Jesus Christ
is the greatest example of principled living and the person he
most admires."

—⁂—

In fact, it is exactly in his ability to set an example that we
may find Bush's greatest strength. He breaks type here as
well. Indeed, in this he is very like George Washington.
Contrary to myth, Washington was not a great military
strategist. He was not the most articulate, the most learned,
or in any way the most gifted man of his time. He was
embarrassed throughout his life both by his lack of education and by his bad teeth, two reasons he seldom smiled and
seldom spoke in public.

Washington exercised a brand of leadership powered by
moral might. He led by character. Men followed him because
they believed the hand of God was upon him and because
they thought him a greater man than they were. He modeled
what they wanted to be and embodied what they hoped
their countrymen would become. He was not perfect. He
was stubborn, had a fierce temper, and possessed a streak of
vanity, but men showed mercy for his flaws because they
hungered to be part of the greatness of his life.

Bush is emerging into this same kind of man. He is learning to shape the prevailing culture of leadership by his example. Two stories reveal this.

Late in 2002, Senator Pete Domenici nominated Judge
Robert Brack for the U.S. District Court in New Mexico. In
February of the next year, Brack attended a judicial review
meeting at the White House. At one point in the discussion,
David Leitch, deputy counsel and deputy assistant to the
president, asked Brack to define his judicial policy. Brack, a

deeply religious man, said, "It can best be defined through the words of the Old Testament prophet Micah: 'What does the Lord require of you, but to act justly, love mercy, and walk humbly with your God?'"[35]

Brack wondered if he had been too outspoken and approached Leitch after the meeting to explain. No need, he discovered. Leitch said that he too was a Christian and that there "wasn't going to be any problem with this president," that in fact he was the very type of person George W. Bush was looking for. Later, Brack heard that when the president looked over the executive summary and read Brack's words, he said, "Oh, I like this. Good stuff."[36]

Men in Washington's camps understood what their commander wanted by the way he lived. It is becoming the same with Bush, so that even the principles of the judicial philosophy he seeks may be divined from the values that he lives.

Another tale: In Walter Reed Medical Center, a soldier is receiving visitors. The young man is in bad shape. His left hand is gone, his face is wired together, and his left side is badly mangled.

The group is there to honor him, but they feel a bit clumsy and unsure. What do you do to honor one so badly wounded? Just then, a member of the group steps forward and shows the way.

Taking the stump of the wounded soldier reverently in his hands, the visitor kneels at the bedside and begins to pray. When he is finished, he stands, kisses the soldier on the head, and tells him that he loves him. The man honoring the soldier is George W. Bush, commander in chief.

This story is circulated around the country by e-mail, and many regard it as another urban legend, part of the mythology that Bush's faith inspires. But this one is true. The wounded soldier is Sergeant Cortinas, and the story is related by Sergeant Major Jack L. Tilley, who had visited the same soldier just a few days before the president and heard the tale from those who were there.[37]

When men and women in the armed forces hear of this episode, it moves them, imparting courage and devotion to a president unashamed to bow by a young man who has suffered doing his bidding. Men in the field turn to each other and comment on what a change this is from recent years, that now they are heroes in the heart of their leader.

And they grow to love him: this flawed Everyman, indefinable commander in chief.

With liberty and justice for all: The president addresses the nation
from Ellis Island on September 11, 2002, the one-year anniversary
of the terrorist attacks on America.

EPILOGUE

To Serve the Present Age

I have the feeling that God has created us and brought us to our present position of power and strength for some great purpose. And up to now we have been shirking it.
—HARRY S. TRUMAN

Whatever else the presidency of George W. Bush imprints on American history, it will at the least have granted the nation an opportunity to rethink the role of religion in its public life. This comes at a strategic moment: when America's most aggressive global enemy claims to take sanction from a religious system, when the nation's most pressing domestic issues are deeply rooted in matters of morality, and when patterns of population growth and immigration are transforming the spiritual landscape of

169

the country. That this timely reappraisal demands a fresh look at the nation's origins only makes the process more promising, for as America examines her present in light of her past, she may gain the wisdom to chart an even nobler future.

When the first English settlers made their homes in the New World, most did so for distinctly religious reasons. The Pilgrims wrote in their Mayflower Compact, for example, that they sailed "for the Glory of God and the Advancement of the Christian Faith."[1] Others, from the Anglicans of Georgia to the Congregationalists of Massachusetts, did the same.

Among the beliefs many of these settlers shared was that the national churches of Europe had made a mockery of pure religion. When time came to design a national government of their own, Americans included in their founding document a First Amendment that guaranteed every citizen the right to worship as he pleased but forbade the federal government from ever establishing a national church. Thus, Congress could neither "make a law respecting an establishment of religion"—meaning a national church—or "prohibiting the free exercise" of religion by an individual.

It meant that men could be as religious as they wanted to be and that even states could be distinctly Christian in their laws, but that the federal government was forbidden to intrude.

Still, the federal government was permitted to encourage religion in general. Chaplains were funded, Bibles were printed, federal buildings were used as churches, missionaries were sent to the Indians—and all at federal expense. Days of prayer and fasting were declared, and speeches on the floor of Congress repeatedly referred to the Christianity of the American people.

Within a century of the nation's birth, the way Americans interpreted the First Amendment began to change dramatically. This was primarily for two reasons. First, patterns of immigration in the post–Civil War years began producing a more religiously diverse population. Second, as the Supreme Court issued rulings intended to apply federal protections to newly freed slaves, it took the First Amendment restrictions that once pertained only to Congress and applied them to the states as well. Before long, school districts and city governments were bound from encouraging religion in any form—a disorienting change from the habits of a century or more.

When the Supreme Court adopted language Thomas Jefferson had used in a private letter and began making rulings in terms of a "wall of separation between church and state," the break from original intent was complete. Soon, practices once commonly understood as bequeaths of a Christian heritage were somehow deemed violations of the new understanding of a secular state. Courts found that the Ten Commandments posted in government buildings, the prayer that started each day in the public schools, the "release time" that permitted students to study their faith during school hours, and even nativity scenes on government grounds were all in violation of First Amendment safeguards.

Accompanying this shift in law was a shift in culture. Government began to be perceived as nonreligious, and elected leaders were expected to follow suit. This meant a change in what men brought from their private lives into public office. That a man was a devoted church member might be celebrated as a reason to vote for him, but he was not supposed to allow what he learned in that church to affect what he did in office.

This produced an odd and somewhat schizophrenic culture. Candidates for office routinely affirmed their faith in God as the most important aspect of their lives, and then all but promised to disregard that God once in office so as not to violate the separation of church and state. In essence, the American electorate was asking candidates for office to sacrifice the most important part of themselves in order to take office. This meant that the nation's leaders had to be the kind of people who could divide themselves neatly between the sacred and the secular.

This new secular orientation prevailed for a season but was already in transition before George W. Bush assumed the presidency. Jimmy Carter's openness about being born again started the change, and the shift continued under Ronald Reagan and Bill Clinton, both of whom were outspoken about their personal faith and the need for religion in public life. With the urging of the Religious Right, the influence of leading religious voices like Billy Graham, and issues like abortion and prayer demanding a moral stand, elected leaders became more vocal about faith and its role in society.

All this set the stage for George W. Bush. He is among a small number of American presidents to have undergone a profound religious transformation as an adult: Andrew Jackson, Abraham Lincoln, and Grover Cleveland were the others. He came to the presidency, then, with the zeal of the newly converted. He also came armed with an understanding of church and state that the Reagan revolution and thinkers on the Religious Right had taught him but which was actually a rephrasing of the traditional understanding of faith and policy.

He was already engineering a religious renovation of the executive branch when the country suffered a traumatic terrorist attack that placed religion unashamedly at the center of American political and social life. The secular state seemed to recede for a time. Congressional leaders sang hymns on the Capitol steps and even introduced legislation to adopt "God Bless America" as the official national hymn.

What followed was a freer reign for religion in American society. Bush seemed to embody it. He prayed publicly and spoke of faith, divine destiny, and the nation's religious heritage more than he ever had. Aides found him facedown on the floor in prayer in the Oval Office. It became known that he refused to eat sweets while American troops were in Iraq, a partial fast seldom reported of an American president. And he framed America's challenges in nearly biblical language. Saddam Hussein is an evildoer. He has to go. There must be a new day in the Middle East. Isaac and Ishmael must shake hands in peace.

Bush's approach to domestic issues sounded a similarly religious tone, an approach he intended as a harkening back to the early understanding of religion and state. So, now, born of crisis, challenge, and a sense that "the commitment of our fathers is now the calling of our time," the nation is forced by the Bush administration to confront its religious direction and diversity.[2] There are questions to be answered. Should a political candidate be required to restrict the implications of his faith to every realm of his life except that of his service to his country? How can a call for returning to the original intent of the First Amendment take into account the religious and demographic transformation of the nation? How can institutions of faith be empowered to do good but kept from engendering religious bigotry and excess?

While these questions are pondered, Bush continues to let faith frame his presidency. Indeed, it seems at times that politics takes a back seat to the religious imprint he hopes to make on the nation. As he told a gathering of ministers in the Oval Office, "I'm not after the votes....I am here, and I am in this room sharing concerns because someday I am going to stand before God, and I want to hear Him say, 'Well done!' I hope that's why we're all here."[3]

—∞—

In the wake of the September 11 disaster, art played a vital role in the nation's process of grieving. One artist in particular seemed to capture what many were feeling in those torturous months. His name was Ron DiCianni, and his paintings of heroic firemen and policemen superimposed over symbols of Americana and faith were widely popular.

In May of 2002, DiCianni gave an exhibition of his work in Midland, Texas, and found himself telling a man who attended the show about his desire to commemorate George W. Bush's leadership after 9/11 with an eye to extolling the president's reliance on prayer. The other man was fascinated and surprised the artist by asking him if he had permission to mention the idea to the president himself. It turned out DiCianni was talking to one of Bush's childhood friends.

Three weeks later, a member of Bush's cabinet called to confirm the president's enthusiastic response to the idea. DiCianni set to work. He decided to portray the president at prayer while leaning against a podium, an image Americans knew well. But at his side would be the clearly discernible figures of Washington and Lincoln, each of whom would also be in prayer while laying a hand upon Bush's shoulder. When DiCianni finished the painting, he learned that the only presidential portraits hanging in the Oval Office were of Lincoln and Washington—a fact he took as confirmation of his design.

The painting symbolizes a large part of the "charge" Bush believes he is keeping. There is, he perceives, a neglected legacy of faith in American history. While it is not his role to preach this faith, it is his role to apply its truth to all he is called to do as chief executive.

And, now, he is not alone. In fact, he may no longer be that lone horseman charging over the hill to his destiny, as depicted in the Koerner painting *A Charge to Keep*. Significantly, that painting no longer hangs in his office. Now he is the bearer of a torch of faith, passed from generations that have come before, both in his own family and in the nation as a whole. He has received an impartation—from God, from heroes past, from the millions who pray for him—and he will fulfill his charge until he hears the words he hopes are said at the end of his days: "Well done."

ACKNOWLEDGMENTS

I have had the privilege of writing this book with some of the finest people I know. To have them as friends is an honor beyond description. To have worked at their side will remain among the dearest memories of my life.

George Grant has given of his astonishing literary genius and historical mastery with both generosity and grace. I am grateful for his investment in this book and, more, for his devoted friendship through the years. In recent months, he has cost me a small fortune in barbecue, but it has been worth every dime.

Eric Holmberg took time away from his award-winning work as a filmmaker and a family life of seeming biblical proportions to do the research that made this book possible. He never complained and never ceased to be a source of wisdom for me. Because of his sardonic wit, we jokingly call him Sardon the Magnificent, but he truly is a magnificent man.

Tony Woodall served as the administrator for this project, and his astonishing array of gifts surprised even me—and I am his biggest fan. He is, to my mind, the perfect southern gentleman: wise, romantic, tender, fierce in battle, deeply mystical, well-mannered, and fun in the fullest Celtic sense. No one makes me laugh like Tony, and I love him for it.

This is the first of my books in which my son, Jonathan Mansfield, has worked at my side. Though only recently graduated from high school, he contributed wisdom beyond his years and an offbeat sense of humor that, unfortunately, he gets from me. Some of the jewels in these pages are his.

The idea for this book came from my friend Stephen Strang. He, along with Barbara Dycus and the dear people of

Strang Communications, has been a wise mentor and understanding comrade. At their side have been Joel Fotinos and Mitch Horowitz of Penguin Group (USA). We have had a great time together, and no author could ask for a better team. I am thankful beyond words and not unaware of what it has meant for them to put up with me.

There have been many kind souls who have talked to us about the president and his faith. Among them are legendary Andover historian Tom Lyons, James Robison, Marvin Olasky, Don Jones, Jim Sale, Arthur Blessitt, James Dobson, Judge Robert Brack, Richard Land, Sergeant Major Jack L. Tilley, Colonel James Henderson, and Ron DiCianni. Their wisdom graces these pages.

I am forever grateful to the Morning Star International family, particularly Rice Broocks, Jim Laffoon, John Rohrer, and Sam Webb, for catching me when I was falling and body checking my soul on more than one occasion. If I become anything near the man I was made to be, it will be in large part due to their tending. Dave Houston and his team provided uniquely strategic support for this project, and I could not have done without the genius of Rick Myers and Sam Chappell, who now run my world—gloriously. Thank you all.

For their unique contributions to my life and this book, for enduring the moments of agony and of triumph, I must offer deepest thanks to my sister, Cindy Lewis, my brother, David Mansfield, Wes and Mary Lamoureux, Beth Moore, Scott Hughes, Robert Zaloba, Ron Cottle, Bill and Lisa Shuler, and Kendall Hewitt.

Finally, among my dearest friends in the world are country music legends Marty and Connie (Smith) Stuart. I do not mention them for their fame, but because when I was in the pit, they spoke tenderly and poetically to me as souls who know the pit well. God, how I love them.

NOTES

Introduction

1. Bill Keller, "God and George W. Bush," *NYTimes.com*, 17 May 2003.

2. George W. Bush, Iowa Debate, Des Moines Civic Center, 13 December 1999.

3. George W. Bush, *A Charge to Keep: My Journey to the White House* (New York: Perennial, 2001), 6.

4. George W. Bush, Inaugural Address, Washington, D.C., 20 January 2001.

5. Ibid.

6. George W. Bush, speech at Islamic Center of Washington, D.C., 17 September 2001.

7. Merle Miller, *Plain Speaking: The Oral Autobiography of Harry Truman* (New York: G. P. Putnam's Sons, 1973), 26.

8. Charles Cecil Wall, *George Washington: Citizen-Soldier* (Charlottesville: University Press of Virginia, 1980), 43.

9. Russell E. Richey, *American Civil Religion* (New York: HarperCollins, 1974).

Chapter 1
A Charge to Keep

1. Mickey Herskowitz, *Duty, Honor, Country* (Nashville: Rutledge Hill Press, 2003), 4.

2. Bush, *A Charge to Keep*, 42–43.

3. Hershowitz, *Duty, Honor, Country*, 4.

4. Ibid., 6.

5. Ibid., 18.

6. Ibid., 19.

7. Ibid., 7

8. Ibid., 22.

9. Ibid., 24.

10. Bill Minutaglio, *First Son: George W. Bush and the Bush Family Dynasty* (New York: Three Rivers Press, 1999), 222.

11. "Rockefeller Under Fire, Bush Urges That He Withdraw," *U.S. News & World Report*, 24 June 1963.

12. Interview notes from Herbert Parmet research; as recorded in Elizabeth Mitchell, *W: Revenge of the Bush Dynasty* (New York: Hyperion, 2000), 66.

13. Matthew Henry, *Matthew Henry's Commentary on the Whole Bible* (Brattleboro: Fessenden and Company, 1835), Vol. 1, 388.

14. "A Charge to Keep I Have," words by Charles Wesley. Public domain. From the Cyerhymnal website: www.cyberhymnal. org/htm/c/h/chargkeep.htm.

15. Bush, *A Charge to Keep*, 45.

Chapter 2
And Manfully to Fight

1. The Episcopal liturgy recounted here in italicized text is from the 1928 edition of the *Book of Common Prayer*, the one used in the baptism of George W. Bush.

2. Doug Wead, *George Bush, Man of Integrity* (Eugene: Harvest House Publishers, 1988), 34.

3. Ibid.

4. Terry Mattingly, "George W. Bush Learns to 'Testify,'" *Scripps Howard News Service*, 17 March 1999.

5. George Bush, Inaugural Address, Washington, D.C., 20 January 1989.

6. Robert H. Schuller, "More Than Conquerors," sermon, 7 October 2001.

7. Wead, *George Bush,* 47.

8. Herskowitz, *Duty, Honor, Country*, 51.

9. Barbara Bush, *Barbara Bush: A Memoir* (New York: St. Martin's Paperbacks, 1995), 229.

10. Ibid., 239.

11. The title of this chapter is taken from the original text of these words found in the 1549 edition of the *Book of Common Prayer*.

12. Herskowitz, *Duty, Honor, Country,* 87.

13. Tony Carnes, "A Presidential Hopeful's Progress," *Christianity Today,* 2 October 2000.

14. Pamela Colloff, "The Son Rises," *Texas Monthly,* June 1999.

15. Bush, *Barbara Bush: A Memoir,* 50.

16. Bush, *A Charge to Keep,* 18.

17. Ibid., 19.

Chapter 3
The Nomadic Years

1. "Excellence and Intensity in U.S. Prep Schools," *Time,* 25 October 1962.

2. Bush, *A Charge to Keep,* 21.

3. Minutaglio, *First Son,* 63–64.

4. Gail Sheehy, "The Accidental Candidate," *Vanity Fair,* October 2000, 174.

5. Ibid.

6. *Harper's Magazine,* July 2000, 20.

7. Florence, SC, 17 February 2000.

8. Sheehy, "The Accidental Candidate," 176.

9. Bush has been dismissive of the charge he might be dyslexic. As he once said in a press conference, "No, I am not dyslexic. I appreciate the diagnosis." ("Bush Touts Health Care Reform in Must-Win Florida," The White House, Office of the Press Secretary, 13 September 2000.)

10. Winston Churchill, *My Early Life: A Roving Commission* (New York: Charles Scribner's Sons, 1930), 13.

11. Sara Rimer, "Teaching as a Torrent of Bubbling Information," *New York Times,* 31 July 1999.

12. Ibid.

13. Theresa Pease, "A Change of Dreams," *Andover Bulletin,* Fall 1997, 10.

14. Rimer, "Teaching as a Torrent of Bubbling Information."

15. Tom Lyons, interview with author, 19 June 2003.

16. Bush, *A Charge to Keep,* 21.

17. Ibid., 19.

18. Sheehy, "The Accidental Candidate," 181.

19. Ron Rosenbaum, "An Elegy for Mumbo Jumbo," *Esquire*, September 1997, 86.

20. Helen Thorpe, "Go East, Young Man," *Texas Monthly*, June 1999.

21. Bush, *A Charge to Keep*, 47.

22. Sam Howe Verhovek, "Is There Room on the Republican Ticket for Another Bush?," *New York Times*, 13 September 1998.

23. Nicholas D. Kristof, "The 2000 Campaign: The Texas Governor; Ally of an Older Generation Amid the Tumult of the 60s," *New York Times*, 19 June 2000.

24. Verhovek, "Is There Room on the Republican Ticket for Another Bush?"

25. Bush, *A Charge to Keep*, 58.

26. Skip Hollandsworth, "Younger. Wilder?" *Texas Monthly*, June 1999.

27. Howard Fineman, "Bush and God," *Newsweek*, 10 March 2003, 26.

28. Minutaglio, *First Son*, 148.

29. Sheehy, "The Accidental Candidate," 181.

30. Bush, *A Charge to Keep*, 60.

31. "Class Day Speaker Gregory Tells Seniors: Something Must Be Wrong with America," *Harvard Crimson*, 12 June 1975; as recorded in Minutaglio, *First Son*, 162.

32. Bush, *A Charge to Keep*, 60.

33. Sam Attlesey, "You Can Take Bush out of Texas...," *Dallas Morning News*, 21 January 2001.

34. The story was first broken by WPXT-TV of Portland, Maine, 2 November 2000.

35. Ibid.

36. Ken Herman, "The Candidates and the Higher Authority," *Houston Post*, 2 October 1994, A1.

37. Mitchell, *W: Revenge of the Bush Dynasty*, 181.

38. Verhovek, "Is There Room on the Republican Ticket for Another Bush?"

39. Ibid.

Chapter 4
Of Men and Mustard Seeds

1. Don Jones, interview with author, 6 June 2003.

2. Bush, *A Charge to Keep*, 136.

3. Ibid., 137.

4. From Arthur Blessitt's website: www.blessitt.com/adventure/ author.html.

5. From the Guinness website: www.guinnessworldrecords. com/ index.asp?id=48617.

6. Arthur Blessitt, interview with author, 30 June 2003.

7. The account of the meeting between Bush, Blessitt, and Sale was taken from Arthur Blessitt's website (www.blessitt.com/ bush.html) and was corroborated and further developed by the author's interviews with Blessitt on 30 June 2003 and Jim Sale on 17 June 2003.

8. From Arthur Blessitt's website: www.blessitt.com/ bush. html.

9. Sale, interview with author.

10. Carnes, "A Presidential Hopeful's Progress."

11. Jones, interview with author.

12. Ibid.

13. Bush, *A Charge to Keep*, 136.

14. Hollandsworth, "Younger. Wilder?"

15. Carnes, "A Presidential Hopeful's Progress."

16. Bush, *A Charge to Keep*, 136.

17. Ibid.

18. Jones, interview with author.

19. Bush, *A Charge to Keep*, 137.

20. Carnes, "A Presidential Hopeful's Progress."

21. Jim Tanner, interview with author, 29 May 2003.

22. Jones, interview with the author.

23. Bush, *A Charge to Keep*, 135.

24. Ibid., 133.

25. Minutaglio, *First Son*, 210.

26. In addition to the examples given on pages 51 and 72 of

this book, see also *A Charge to Keep*, page 135.

27. Verhovek, "Is There Room on a Republican Ticket for Another Bush?"

28. David Frum, *The Right Man: The Surprise Presidency of George W. Bush* (New York: Random House, 2003), 283.

Chapter 5
"My Faith Frees Me"

1. Bush, *A Charge to Keep*, 6.

2. Minutaglio, *First Son*, 204.

3. Lois Romano and George Lardner Jr., "A Life-Changing Year; Epiphany Fueled Candidate's Climb," *Washington Post*, 25 July 1999, A-1.

4. Ibid.

5. Evan Smith, "George, Washington," *Texas Monthly*, June 1999.

6. Nicholas D. Kristof, "Governor Bush's Journey: The 1988 Campaign for Bush, Thrill Was in Father's Chase," *New York Times*, 29 August 2000.

7. Ibid.

8. Bush, *A Charge to Keep*, 178–179.

9. David Remnick, "Why Is Lee Atwater So Hungry?," *Esquire*, December 1986.

10. Lois Romano and George Lardner Jr., "Bush's Move Up to the Majors," *Washington Post*, 31 July 1999, A-1.

11. Fineman, "Bush and God," 27.

12. J. Lee Grady, "The Faith of George W. Bush," *Charisma & Christian Life*, November 2000, 48.

13. Minutaglio, *First Son*, 213.

14. Smith, "George, Washington."

15. Romano and Lardner Jr., "Bush's Move Up to the Majors."

16. Terence Hunt, "Bush Says 'Gears Shift Tonight,' Staff Faces Quayle-Guard Issue," *Associated Press*, 18 August 1988.

17. Minutaglio, *First Son*, 232.

18. Bush, *A Charge to Keep*, 207.

19. Ibid.

20. George F. Will, *Men at Work* (New York: HarperPerennial, 1991), 2.

21. Bush, *A Charge to Keep*, 199.

22. Ibid., 201.

23. Verhovek, "Is There Room on a Republican Ticket for Another Bush?"

24. Ibid.

25. Sheehy, "The Accidental Candidate," 169.

26. Minutaglio, *First Son*, 244.

27. Ann Richards, speech at the Democratic National Convention, Atlanta, Georgia, 18 July 1988.

28. Romano and Lardner Jr., "Bush's Move Up to the Majors."

29. Ibid.

30. Ibid.

31. Verhovek, "Is There Room on a Republican Ticket for Another Bush?"

32. Romano and Lardner Jr., "Bush's Move Up to the Majors."

33. Herman, "The Candidates and the Higher Authority."

34. Ibid.

35. Verhovek, "Is There Room on a Republican Ticket for Another Bush?"

36. Herman, "The Candidates and the Higher Authority," A-1, A-21.

37. Bush, *A Charge to Keep*, 37.

38. Ibid., 40.

39. Tucker Carlson, "Devil May Care," *Talk*, September 1999, 106. Whether Bush ever said those words or used that tone has been strongly disputed. Quite a few friends and coworkers, most notably Don Jones, Karen Hughes, and Doug Wead, have spoken passionately about how the governor agonized over the Karla Faye Tucker case.

40. Citizens United for Alternatives to the Death Penalty, www.cuadp.org/bush.html.

41. Carnes, "A Presidential Hopeful's Progress."

42. Marvin Olasky, editorial, *Wall Street Journal*, 15 August 1995, A-16.

43. Marvin Olasky, "Compassionate Conservation," *Veritas—A Quarterly Journal of Public Policy in Texas*, Fall 2000, 7–8.

44. Carnes, "A Presidential Hopeful's Progress."

45. Bush, *A Charge to Keep*, 6.

Chapter 6
To Build a House of Faith

1. J. Lee Grady, "The Spiritual Side of Al Gore," *Charisma & Christian Life*, November 2000, 49.

2. Al Gore, speech to Salvation Army's Adult Rehabilitation Center, Atlanta, Georgia, 25 May 1999.

3. Grady, "The Spiritual Side of Al Gore."

4. Ceci Connolly, "Gore Urges Role for 'Faith-Based' Groups," *Washington Post*, 25 May 1999.

5. Gore, speech to Salvation Army.

6. Connolly, "Gore Urges Role for 'Faith-Based' Groups."

7. Sheehy, "The Accidental Candidate."

8. Ibid.

9. Frum, *The Right Man*, 79.

10. Bush, *A Charge to Keep*, 8.

11. Ibid., 9.

12. Carnes, "A Presidential Hopeful's Progress."

13. James Robison, interview with author, tape recording, Dallas, Texas, 28 May 2003.

14. Robison, interview with author.

15. Ibid.

16. Ibid.

17. Ibid.

18. Ibid.

19. Ibid.

20. Ibid.

21. Ibid.

22. Keith Butler, interview with Stephen Strang, 28 August 2003.

23. Grady, "The Faith of George W. Bush," 50.

24. Ibid.

25. Verhovek, "Is There Room on a Republican Ticket for Another Bush?"

26. Robison, interview with author.

27. John McCain, press conferences aboard the Straight Talk Express, February 28 & 29, 2000.

28. Joe Klein, "The Blinding Glare of His Certainty," *Time*, 24 February 2003.

29. Frum, *The Right Man*, 9.

30. Ibid.

31. Ibid.

32. Stephen Ambrose, *To America: Personal Reflections of an Historian* (New York: Simon & Schuster, 2002), 3.

33. George W. Bush, Inaugural Address, Washington, D.C., 20 January 2001.

34. Peggy Noonan, "Farewell," *Wall Street Journal*, 19 April 2001.

35. Tom Raum, "Bush Acting to Block Last-Minute Clinton Rules," *Associated Press*, 20 January 2001.

36. Frum, *The Right Man*, 79.

37. Ron Suskind, "Mrs. Hughes Takes Her Leave," *Esquire*, 138, no. 1, July 2002.

38. Frum, *The Right Man,* 1.

39. White House, Guidelines on Religious Exercise and Religious Expression in the Federal Workplace, 14 August 1997.

40. [John Doe], interview with author, 16 May 2003.

41. Frum, *The Right Man*, 16.

42. Ibid., 14.

43. Kenneth T. Walsh, "A Sunday Service in the Air," *U.S. News and World Report*, 19 May 2003, 32.

44. Oswald Chambers, *My Utmost for His Highest* (New York: Dodd, Mead & Company, 1935), 246, 1.

45. What follows is taken from the speech given to the American Jewish Committee, National Building Museum, Washington, D.C., 3 May 2001.

46. Quoted in John Eidsmoe, *The Christian Legal Advisor* (Milford, Conn.: Mott Media, 1984), 133–164.

47. Frum, *The Right Man*, 253.

48. Pat Buchanan, *McLaughlin Group*, 15 June 1990.

49. The discussion over violence and tolerance within the world of Islam is both ancient and voluminous. Several recent books explore the complex issue of whether faithful Muslims can coexist with Jews and Christians—to say nothing of tolerating the existence of Israel over the long term. For further information, see: R. C. Sproul and Abdul Saleeb, *The Dark Side of Islam* (Wheaton, Ill.: Crossway Books, 2003); Bernard Lewis, *What Went Wrong? The Clash of Islam and Modernity* (New York: Perennial Press, 2003); Bernard Lewis, *The Crisis of Islam: Holy War and Unholy Terror* (New York: Modern Library, 2003); George Grant, *Blood of the Moon: The Historic Conflict Between Islam and Western Civilization* (Nashville: Thomas Nelson, 2002).

Chapter 7
A New Day of Infamy

1. Michael Kranish, "Bush: U.S. to Hunt Down the Attackers," *Boston Globe*, 11 September 2001.

2. Ibid.

3. "President Bush's Activities During Day of Crisis," *Associated Press*, 12 September 2001.

4. "Remarks by the President Upon Arrival at Barksdale Air Force Base," Barksdale Air Force Base, Louisiana (the White House, Office of the Press Secretary), 11 September 2001.

5. Frum, *The Right Man*, 119.

6. "President Bush's Activities During Day of Crisis," *Associated Press*.

7. Frum, *The Right Man*, 121.

8. Ibid., 120.

9. "President Bush's Activities During Day of Crisis," *Associated Press*.

10. "Statement by the President in His Address to the Nation"

(the White House, Office of the Press Secretary), 11 September 2001.

11. Frum, *The Right Man*, 128.

12. Chambers, My *Utmost for His Highest*, 255.

13. Ibid.

14. "Remarks by the President in Photo Opportunity with the National Security Team," Cabinet Room (the White House, Office of the Press Secretary), 12 September 2001.

15. Stephen Mansfield, *Never Give In: The Extraordinary Character of Winston Churchill* (Nashville: Cumberland House, 1996), 32.

16. "Remarks by the President in Photo Opportunity with the National Security Team," Cabinet Room (the White House, Office of the Press Secretary), 12 September 2001.

17. Dan Balz, Bob Woodward, and Jeff Himmelman, "10 Days in September: Inside the War Cabinet; Afghan Campaign's Blueprint Emerges," *Washington Post*, 29 January 2002, A-1.

18. "President's Remarks at National Day of Prayer and Remembrance," the National Cathedral, Washington, D.C. (the White House, Office of the Press Secretary), 14 September 2001.

19. Ibid.

20. Ibid.

21. Ibid.

22. "Remarks by the President to Police, Firemen, and Rescue Workers," Murray and West Streets, New York, New York (the White House, Office of the Press Secretary), 14 September 2001.

23. Frum, *The Right Man*, 141.

24. "Remarks by the President at Islamic Center of Washington, D.C." (the White House, Office of the Press Secretary), 17 September 2001.

25. Douglas Layton, doctor of Islamic studies, author of *Deceiving a Nation: Islam in America*, interview with author, 15 June 2003.

26. President Bush's address to a joint session of Congress, 20 September 2001.

27. Sheikh Hamza Yusuf, speech at benefit dinner titled "Justice for Imam Jamil Al-Amin," University of California—Irvine, 9 September 2001.

28. "Remarks by the President Upon Arrival," the South Lawn (the White House, Office of the Press Secretary), 16 September 2001.

29. Grover Norquist, "The Natural Conservatives: Muslims deliver for the GOP," *American Spectator*, June 2001.

30. Bill Broadway, "God's Place on the Dais," *Washington Post*, 27 January 2001, B-9.

31. Franklin Graham, interview at the dedication of a chapel in Wilkesboro, N.C., October 2001.

32. Franklin Graham, interview with NBC, 16 November 2001.

33. Franklin Graham, "My View of Islam," *Wall Street Journal*, 9 December 2001.

34. Ibid.

35. Todd Starnes, "Graham Stands by Statement Calling Islam 'Wicked, Violent,'" *Worthy News*, 19 November 2001.

36. Jerry Falwell, *60 Minutes* interview, 6 October 2002.

37. Pat Robertson, *The 700 Club*, 11 November 2002.

38. "Remarks by President George W. Bush in a statement to reporters during a meeting with U.N. Secretary General Kofi Annan," the Oval Office, Washington, D.C. (the White House, Office of the Press Secretary), 13 November 2002.

39. President Bush's address to a joint session of Congress, 20 September 2001.

40. St. Augustine, *The City of God* (New York: Doubleday, 1958), 447.

41. Ibid.

42. Jimmy Carter, "Just War—Or a Just War?," *New York Times*, 9 March 2003.

43. Susan B. Thistlethwaite, "President Bush's War Against Iraq Is Not a 'Just War,'" *Chicago Tribune*, 15 October 2002.

44. Kathryn Jean Lopez, "Justice in War: Just-War Theory," *National Review Online*, 15 October 2001.

45. Michael Novak, "'Asymmetrical Warfare' & Just War: A Moral Obligation," *National Review Online*, 10 February 2003.

46. Norman Podhoretz, "How to Win World War IV," *Commentary* 113 (February 2002): 19, 11.

47. "Bush calls Saddam 'the Guy Who Tried to Kill My Dad,'" John King, *CNN*, 27 September 2002, Posted: 1:48 AM EDT.

Chapter 8
Bush Unbound

1. Frum, *The Right Man*, 79.

2. George W. Bush, speech at Goree Island, Senegal, 8 July 2003.

3. Condoleezza Rice, *Meet the Press*, 9 September 2001.

4. Annual dinner of the White House Correspondents Association, Washington Hilton, 4 May, 2002.

5. Ibid.

6. David Margolick, "Blair's Big Gamble," *Vanity Fair*, June 2003, 226.

7. Julia Campbell, "Where Will He Stand?: Bush Faces Difficult Issues on Gay Rights," abcNEWS.com, 17 January 2001.

8. Lou Chibbaro Jr., "Mixed Reviews on Lesbian and Gay Rights for Bush's First Year," *Rights at Risk: Equality in an Age of Terrorism* (Report by Citizens' Commission on Civil Rights, 2002), chapter 15.

9. Christopher Hitchens, "God and Man in the White House," *Vanity Fair*, August 2003, 81.

10. John Ashcroft, commencement address at Bob Jones University, 8 May 1999.

11. Hitchens, "God and Man in the White House," 76, 78.

12. John Ashcroft, speech to the Detroit Economics Club, November 1988.

13. George Bush, town hall meeting in Ontario, California, 5 January 2002.

14. James Robison, interview with author, 29 June 2003.

15. Kristof, "The 2000 Campaign: The Texas Governor; Ally of an Older Generation Amid the Tumult of the 60s."

16. Margolick, "Blair's Big Gamble," 223.

17. Mitchell, *W: Revenge of the Bush Dynasty*, 217.

18. Ibid.

19. White House remarks on AIDS proposal, 31 January 2003.

20. Nicholas D. Kristof and Frank Bruni, "The Republicans:

Man in the News; A Confident Son of Politics Rises," *New York Times*, 3 August 2000.

21. James Moore and Wayne Slater, *Bush's Brain* (New York: John Wiley and Sons, 2003).

22. Richard Land, interview with author, 3 June 2003.

23. Robison, interview with author, 29 June 2003.

24. John J. DiIulio Jr., "Not a Leap of Faith," *Weekly Standard*, 30 June 2003.

25. Ibid.

26. Robert G. Kaiser, "Bush and Sharon Nearly Identical on Mideast Policy," *Washington Post*, 9 February 2003, A-1.

27. Gordon Corera, "Abbas Wins White House Red Carpet," BBC News, 25 July 2003.

28. Tucker Carlson, "The Politics of Virtue," *City Journal* 8, no. 3, Summer 1998.

29. Interview with British paper *Scotland on Sunday*, quoted in Jo Thomas, "Governor Bush's Journey: A Man Adrift," *New York Times*, 22 July 2000.

30. Romano and Lardner Jr., "1986: A Life-Changing Year; Epiphany Fueled Candidate's Climb."

31. Ibid.

32. George W. Bush, speech to the Northern White Mountain Chamber of Commerce, Gorham, New Hampshire, 2 November 1999.

33. Ann Gerhart, "Jenna Bush Is Fined, Loses Driver's License," *Washington Post*, 7 July 2001, C-3; "Bush Girls Face Court Over Drink Violations," *News Letter*, 2 June 2001.

34. Gavin Ewards, "Ashton Kutcher," *Rolling Stone*, 29 May 2003, 46.

35. Micah 6:8.

36. Robert Brack, interview with author, 2 July 2003.

37. Sergeant Major Tilley, interview with author, 1 July 2003.

Epilogue
To Serve the Present Age

1. *Mayflower Compact*, 11 November 1620 as quoted in

William Bradford, *Of Plymouth Plantation 1620–1647* (New York: Alfred A. Knopf, 1997), 76.

2. President's Remarks at National Day of Prayer and Remembrance, the National Cathedral, Washington, D.C. (the White House, Office of the Press Secretary), 14 September 2001.

3. James Robison, interview with author, 24 June 2003.

INDEX